GRANDDAUGHTER, LET'S TALK ABOUT MONEY

Plain talk about finances, updated 2022.

By Edd Breeden

Online, www.breeden.us

Email edd@breeden.us

Second Edition, 2022

Scripture quotations are original renditions by the author.

ISBN 9798616804631

For my grandchildren:

Marcus, because he asked the question,

And for Nate, Carleigh, Corry,

Kennedy, James, Hollie,

Suzie Mae, and Lucas.

OTHER BOOKS BY EDD BREEDEN

Available in paperback and digital format.

- **Autobiographical**
  - The Drunken Preacher
  - Grandson, Let's Talk about Money
  - Granddaughter, Let's Talk about Money
- **Finances**
  - Church Treasurer's Manual (PCUSA)
  - The Handbook for Church Treasurers
  - The Volunteer's Audit Guide for Churches and Other Non-Profits
  - Money, Money, Money, vol. 1 and 2
- **Christian Living Titles.**
  - Discipleship Training Manual.
  - Generous Living, Jesus Teaches about Wealth.
    - Vol. 1, Matthew. & Vol. 2, Matthew.
  - Prayer, A Practical Guide to Spending Time with God.
  - Unmasked and Loved, A Resource for Peer-Counselors, Co-Authored with the late Zelpha Blythe-Persson.
- **Commentaries.**
  - 40 Mornings with the Apostle John, A Study of the Revelations 1-5.
  - Ephesians Amplified.
  - Galatians Amplified.
  - Philippians Amplified.
- **Study Guides, Bible Studies.**
  - Advent Study Guides.
- **Pastor Helps.**
  - Christmas Eve Candlelight Service.
  - Christmas Sermons, Vol. 1 and Vol. 2
  - Worship Services for Special Occasions, Baker House Publishers, out of print.

ABOUT THE AUTHOR, EDD BREEDEN

Edd received his Bachelor's Degree in Mathematics from the University of California at Santa Barbara in 1970 and a Master of Divinity degree from Fuller Theological Seminary, Pasadena, CA. in 1974. Having always been interested in personal and church finances, he went to work for investment firms in the late 1990's as a financial advisor. In the early 2000's he became a registered tax preparer. As the treasurer of the Presbytery of San Jose, he attended a number of financial conferences and began to write books and teach seminars for church treasurers.

He has also pastored Presbyterian Churches in Minnesota and California. His emphasis in seminary centered on Biblical languages and Bible Study and has continued through the years to seek a deeper understanding of the Scriptures. This led to his interest in what the Bible had to say about money. After many years of study, he has recently written Money, Money, Money, what the New Testament says about money.

He lives in Scotts Valley, CA, with his wife. Married in 1968, they have four children and 9 living grandchildren and love spending time with family and friends.

He loves to write, teach, read, play golf, and listen to Country Western Music.

GRANDDAUGHTER, LET'S TALK ABOUT MONEY

Plain talk about finances.

By Edd Breeden

Online, www.breeden.us

Email edd@breeden.us

Forward

In a conversation with my grandson, Marcus, and one of his friends, the topic of money came up. They started asking questions that I could easily see would take more than a 10-minute conversation to answer. When the conversation was over, there was so much more I wanted them to learn to avoid the pitfalls I had experienced in my life.

Just knowing the right thing to do does not mean you will do the right thing. But if you do not know the right thing it is only by chance that you can do something the best way. So, here are the things I have learned along the way. What you do with it is up to you.

I would like all my grandchildren, as well as other young people to know about the basics of handling money. This book covers where you get money, how you spend it, what you own and what you owe, and why it helps to know all this early in life. I have also included information on record keeping, managing your bank accounts, taxes, and the benefits of giving money away, saving money, investing money and budgeting. One chapter looks at the benefits and hindrances of having any kind of debt and another chapter talks about protecting your wealth with insurance and trusts. And for those who are interested in starting their own business/hobby on the side, I included some basic principles of how to make your business successful and last more than 5 years.

I hope you enjoy the read. Papa.

This Page Intentionally Left Blank

TABLE OF CONTENTS

This Page Intentionally Left Blank

Chapter One;

The Richest Man in Babylon

Set Aside Something from Every Paycheck

Years ago, I ran across a very small book entitled, "The Richest Man in Babylon," by George S. Clason. I only remember one thing from the book. I know it contained more advice than what I took away from it, but, the core thought spinning in my head when the book was over was this; For every 10 coins you put into your pocket only take out 9. Or, for every $100 you take home from work, only spend $90, and save the rest.

In essence, save ten percent of everything you make. Or, as my father told me, set aside something from every "paycheck."

I will give you some ideas later, on what it means to save and what you should be saving for, but for now, just remember this one principle: For every 10 coins you put in your pocket, only take out 9.

Over the years, with a wife, kids, hobbies, and houses, saving 10 percent of every paycheck did not work well for me. But the idea has stuck with me and I have been able to have a comfortable life. Always strive to put ten percent away into your "savings.".

The day Linda and I got engaged in 1967, my father offered some great advice. Similar to the "richest man in Babylon," he said, "Save five dollars from every paycheck." I was making about $2.00 an hour at the time, so he was suggesting I save about 6% of every paycheck. I did not follow his advice.

Another way to say it is this: Never spend more than you make. There is always a temptation to spend more than you have. The pressure comes from friends, from advertising, from spouses and close friends, and even from deep within yourself. Whether you want more for pleasure or for some weird social status with your friends, always put some money away for another time, a very long time away from now. I'll try to tell you why later in the book.

Now, before I leave this thought, remember, a "paycheck" is any source of money that comes your way. You work and get a paycheck; set some aside. You get a bonus at work, do not spend it all, put some of it in your savings. Grandma gives you a gift of cash for your birthday, even with this, put some of your gift into a savings pile, do not spend it all. If you work in a service industry, take some of your tips and put them away for later in life. Even if you sell your car or guitar or your old iPad, however you get money, do not spend all you get.

How much should you save? There is no magical number that works for everyone. Do you save one coin for every ten; 10%? How about the equivalent of $5 per paycheck back in 1968? That would be 6%. Maybe for you, it is just $5 per "paycheck." That is your call but save something from every bit of revenue you receive. And the sooner you start the more you can take advantage of something called "the time value of money."

The Time Value of Money

If you put an amount of money aside every "paycheck" and you "invest" it to receive some level of interest, soon the interest will start earning interest of its own; i.e., your money will be "working for you." The pool of money called your savings will actually become a source of income for you: I call that passive income because you do not have to do much to get it, just put it into the savings and let someone pay you for the privilege of using your money. Over time, if you stay focused your money will make enough money for you that you will not need to work unless you want to. It just takes a little time and a lot of focus.

Think about this idea. If you put a penny in a bank today and two pennies tomorrow and four pennies the next day, and 8 pennies the day after that and keep doubling the number of pennies each day for a month, how much money will you have in 31 days? Take a guess and then go figure it out. You will be surprised at how much money you will accumulate by doubling the amount of money you put in savings every day for a month, starting with just one penny.

If you do the calculations you will see a very simple flaw in the plan, soon you will not be able to double yesterday's amount, it will just be too much money to come up with in one day. However, if you invest your money that you put into savings and receive a reasonable rate on investment (ROI) on your money, your account will grow in value. This will be slow growth at first but in the long run, you will be amazed at how fast the account will grow.

As you go along, the amount of interest you gain is interest on both the Principle, what you have put into the account, and on the Accumulated Interest, the money you have earned. The money you put into the account as you go along is money from Active Income (because you spent hours making the money) and the interest earned is Passive Income (because you did not have to "work" for it.) As the interest starts making more interest, you are using "someone else's money" to generate money for you.

For instance, at a growth rate of 5% per year, $ 1,000 grows to $ 1,600 in 10 years, $2,600 in 20 years, $4,300 in 30 years, $7,000 in 40 years and $11,000 in 50 years. And that is without adding anything to the original $1,000 except the interest. If you add $1,200 per year or about $50 per paycheck you will change those numbers to $16,000 in 10 years, $42,000 in 20 years, $84,000 in 30 years, $152,000 in 40 years and $263,000 in 50 years. And you will have only contributed $61,000; the rest is interest.

Maybe now you will understand the rational of the IRS in limiting the amount of money you can contribute to an IRA or a Roth IRA to a few thousand dollars a year. If you start now and never stop adding to the program, over time, you will amass a large sum of money. The biggest benefit and at the same the hardest things to do is start now and continue to add new money every month.

The Rule of 72

Before I move on to other thoughts let me teach you something called “the Rule of 72.” If you take the annual interest rate you are earning in your saving account and divide that number into 72, the result is how many years it will take for your money to double in value. At 6% annual interest it takes 12 years (72/6=12) for your money to double in value. So, $1,000 becomes $2,000 after 12 years when it is invested at a 6% interest rate. If you invest at 12% interest, it only takes 6 years for your money to double in value. Whatever the interest rate you are getting, you can use the Rule of 72 to estimate how long it will take for your investment to grow to twice as much.

At that time, your interest gained will equal your original investment. And your investment will grow more quickly into the future because you are using your Principle and someone else’s interest to make money for you.

“I Have Never Moved”

I have moved a lot in my life, but my friend Dick has never moved. He grew up in his parents’ home. One day his parents died, and he inherited the house, the ranch, and a whole lot more. When I met Dick, he owned several hundred acres in great ranch land. He still drove the old Mercedes he inherited from his parents. The house had not been remodeled or changed in any major way. But his ranch was four times the size of his parent's land.

One day I said to Dick, "You are a wealthy man." He said, "No, I have never moved." Since he never had a house payment and his property taxes were very low, he had more money than most people to spend or invest. Every time the economy slowed down and his neighbors could not afford the payments on their land and needed to sell, Dick would buy up some more land.

Land is also a form of savings since you acquire the land at a certain price and you later can sell it for a profit, a gain on your original investment. And if you can rent the land or the property out while you wait for the land to go up in value, you benefit just that much more.

Learn from Those you Value.

You know plenty of people you think are doing things right. Spend time with them, interview then, seek from them the secrets of becoming wealthy. In most cases, their success was not just luck, it was diligently sticking to the plan of saving one coin from every 10 coins they received. Whether your learning comes from a book you read or a personal interview, begin now, become a learner and more than that become a saver.

Chapter Two;

Rich Dad Poor Dad

What I Learned from The Book by That Title

Just before the year 2000, at the age of 53, I learned a very important lesson from a book by Robert Kiyosaki, "Rich Dad, Poor Dad." Based upon his own life story he talked about the need for people to be financially literate.

I graduated from college thirty years before I read the book. My major was Mathematics. I did my own tax returns, always balanced my checkbook, had an investment account where I could buy and sell stocks. I wondered what I could learn that I did not already know. It turns out; I learned a lot of new and fascinating things from that book.

My favorite line from the book, that I have quoted often, especially to those talking about going into business was, "anybody can make a better hamburger than McDonalds." Having a great product does not mean you will be a successful business owner. I will share with you more about starting your own business later in this book; but from the book Rich Dad, Poor Dad I learned a lot about basic finances. It all started with the Four Quadrants of Money.

The Four Quadrants of Money

When you ask a person about their money, they might tell you about their income; how much they make. Or, sometimes they will talk about their expenses; usually how much everything costs. Seldom does someone talk about the amount of money they have in their accounts or the amounts they owe someone else.

Your neighbor or friend might drive a very expensive car and act like they have a lot of money. You cannot tell from that whether they are rich or poor; they might just be pretending to have wealth but in reality, they owe the banks more than they can ever pay back.

Without looking at a person's whole financial picture you cannot see the complete financial situation or the financial state of a person. Whenever you ask a bank for a loan, they will ask you to list four things: your income, your monthly expenses, the value of your house and cars, and the amount of money you owe to other banks or people. They do not ask you to put it in the form of the chart on the next page, but without knowing your whole financial picture they cannot determine how much money they can safely loan to you and be able to reasonably expect you to pay it back. Banks try very hard not to make bad loans.

Robert Kiyosaki drew a similar diagram in his book. The chart on the next page is my version of Robert's thinking when I am sitting with someone and talking about their financial situation. I will draw this on a napkin or piece of paper to help them understand the flow of money in their life.

Income	Assets
Expenses	Liabilities

These are the four quadrants that make up a person's whole financial picture. Income is the money you receive, and Expenses is the money you spend. You either spend it to live or you spend it to buy something. If the something you buy has lasting value, it is an Asset. If you borrow money to buy your Asset, you have a Liability; you owe someone something.

Money flows in and out of these boxes, quadrants, on a regular basis. Understanding the flow of money helps you make wise decisions about your current and future financial situation. If you do not pay attention to flow of your money you are not alone, because most people never think about this; they just know that they get money and they spend money.

But before I talk more about the flow of money it is important to talk about your financial statements.

Financial Statements

The chart below has 2 more boxes. Each column now has a heading. This shows two sides of the financial picture of any person or business; The Profit & Loss Statement and the Balance Sheet.

The Profit & Loss Statement	The Balance Sheet
Income	Assets
Expenses	Liabilities

The Profit and Loss Statement talks about how much money you take in, your Income, and how much money you spend, your Expenses. The Balance Sheet shows how much money you have in your bank accounts and your physical Assets, like houses and cars. And it shows how much money you owe to other people or institutions, your Liabilities.

These two documents are often used in businesses to know the value or success of the company. And comparing them from month to month and year to year, you can tell if the business is growing or losing ground financially. A business also must provide these two reports to a bank when they are asking for a loan.

Every time you, as an individual, seek a mortgage or choose to buy something on time, the lender asks you for your financial statements, they just do not call it that. But they ask for the information anyway. You will see this by all the questions they ask on the loan application. Once you understand these four quadrants of money you will recognize what the bank is asking for on the loan application.

When a bank asks a business owner for the financial statements of the business, the business gives the banker a copy of their Profit and Loss Statement and a copy of their Balance Sheet. From these two documents the banker can see how the business makes money (Income), how it spends money (Expenses), the value of the business's accounts and other Assets (Assets), and how much the business owes to someone else (Liabilities).

If an individual printed a Profit and Loss Statement for their personal finances, it would list all the ways the individual received income and how much they received over a period; of say one year or one quarter of a year. As well it would list out all the ways the individual spent or expensed their money. The bottom line of the Profit and Loss Statement shows whether, for any time period, the individual's income was greater than expenses or less than expenses.

If an individual printed out a Balance Sheet for their personal finances, it should list all the bank accounts, investment accounts, and other Assets like houses and cars owned by the individual, provided they entered this information into the financial software program. It would also list all the loans and other liabilities that the individual owed to others; car loans, mortgages, credit card balances, etc. The bottom line of the Balance Sheet shows the Net Worth of the individual at that point in time. (Net Worth = Assets – Liabilities)

Most individuals do not look at their Balance Sheet and if they do, they do not always list all the Assets and liabilities on it. To be very accurate the value of your house should be listed along with the other Assets and your loan against the house should be listed in the Liability section. Likewise, you should list out the value of cars, all your furniture, and even your jewelry and other valuables. Your credit cards would be listed as liabilities because everything you owe on your credit cards is something you would need to pay off right away if you chose to liquidate all your holdings at any particular time.

In the next four chapters of the book I will explain my understanding of the four quadrants; Income, Expenses, Assets, and Liabilities. I will also lay out for you how each of these four categories of money can be used to build a financial base that frees you up to live life to the fullest. First let me share with you how money flows through these quadrants.

The Flow of Money

Money flows into your possession and then flows out again. If you do what I suggested in the first chapter, you would not let everything that flows in, flow out again. You would put some of your money into an Asset called a savings account before you let the rest of the money flow out.

Money flows in from a variety of Income sources and flows out through your expenses. When more money flows in than flows out, you have money to set aside and increase your Assets. Or, let me suggest, as did the Richest Man in Babylon, you put the one coin into the savings before you start spending the other nine.

Those who save money regularly, have a chance to increase their Assets. A long-term goal, for good financial management, is to have more and more Assets that generate income for you, what are often called Income Generators. When you have Income Generators besides your job, you will have money flowing in that you did not "have to work for." That is called Passive Income.

If your work, your business, and your Assets were all flowing money into your Income quadrant of the diagram and some of that income, i.e. the excess of income over expenses, was flowing back to the Assets to help generate more income, can you see that over time, you could accumulate enough Income Generating Assets so you would no longer have to work at a "normal" job?

At your retirement the diagram might look like:

The Profit & Loss Statement	The Balance Sheet
Income from Assets	Income Generators
Expenses	Minimized Liabilities

However, in the meantime your chart will be a bit more cluttered.

The Profit & Loss Statement	The Balance Sheet
Active Income: Work Passive Income: Savings	Bank Accounts Physical Assets Income Generators
Necessary Expenses Optional Expenses	Liabilities: money you owe Liabilities: money you borrow to make money

Your goal from now until you retire is to create Income Generators that will benefit you later in life; i.e. save your money and invest well.

Chapter Three;

Sources of Income or "Getting Money"

The Profit & Loss Statement	The Balance Sheet
Active Income: Work Passive Income: Savings	Income Generators Non-Income Generators
Necessary Expenses Optional Expenses	Liabilities: money you owe Liabilities: money you borrow to make money

The Way the US Government Looks at Income

According to the annual Tax Return Form 1040, which the IRS uses to track our taxable income, an individual has seven distinct sources of income.

Wages or work. (Active Income) A person goes out and finds a job and the employer pays the worker a certain wage for the work done. Some get paid hourly, some get a salary, some might even get a bonus or a commission for their efforts. These are all forms of wages. You put in the time and effort and your employer compensates you with your "paycheck." These wages are usually reported to you on a document called a W-2 form that comes sometime in late January or early February each year if you were employed for some period during the previous year. You will report this income on your tax return as wages and it will begin to form your total taxable income.

It is important for all employees to notice what makes the difference between their gross pay and their net pay. If you work 40 hours for $20 per hour, your paycheck will have a gross pay of $800. But that is not what you take home. That $800 will be reduced by Fed and possibly State withholding. These are monies these governmental agencies take out of your paycheck as a down payment on the taxes you might owe at the end of the year. There will also be a reduction of 7.65% for Social Security and Medicare payments that will help to provide for your retirement and healthcare when you reach the age of 65. Depending on the size of your immediate family, i.e., spouse, kids, etc. your withholding might be different from someone who works with you. But, you will probably see your $800 reduced to $650 before you get your check.

Three successful tips to help you be an employee that is noticed by the bosses and therefore has a higher chance of advancement in the company are these: Show up Early to your job (at least 10-15 minutes), Leave a Little Late (stay 10-15 minutes longer) and from time to time, Ask your supervisor if there is anything else you can do for them. You will probably be the last person your supervisor wants to fire rather than the first. And you will be the first person your supervisor wants to promote or give a raise.

I was listening to a talk show on the radio one day and the guest said there are three goals of a good employee:

> Out Hustle your co-workers in every way, not for the purpose of making them look bad or putting them down, just set your standard to work a little faster and harder than others.
>
> Show up to work. Physically show up to work, on time and stay the whole workday. Do not look for excuses to not work, to leave work, or to avoid work. Emotionally show up as well. Come to work ready to do the job with a positive attitude. Even if you would rather be somewhere else, your obligation is to your employer and the job.
>
> And Excel at doing the job you have been hired to do. Whatever task the owner or your supervisor asks you to do, do it to the best of

your ability. If you are not sure how to do that, aske someone to teach you.

Investment Income, Interest or Dividends. (Passive Income) When you invest money you usually receive a return on your investment (ROI). Investments, which are listed on your Balance Sheet as Assets, can be a wide number of vehicles where you give somebody money in exchange for their promise to pay you a certain rate of annual interest or a regular dividend until they give you your money back. These could be savings accounts, CDS, bonds, stocks, mutual funds, etc. When you receive the regular interest and dividend payments, this money is income to you, even if you just keep the money in the account where the investment is (i.e. reinvest it). In the future, you will begin to draw money out of the investments rather than have them reinvest, but for now, just let it help you grow your Income Generator.

The interest or dividends you receive each month or year is actually added income to you, at least on the IRS 1040 tax return. If you reinvest the interest or dividend you are choosing to receive the income and add it straight back into your savings, either back into the same investment or into another one. Even though you are reinvesting your interest and dividends they are considered taxable income by the IRS in the year you earn them and must be reported on your tax return.

Investment Income, Capital gains from Stocks or Property. (Passive Income) When your Investment Asset does more than pay you interest or dividends, but also has the possibility of increasing in value, you might end up with Capital Gains or Losses. An Investment like this means you have a greater opportunity to lose your money, your Investment, but you gain the ability to receive a potentially higher rate of return on your Investment. You might expect to gain some interest or some dividends, but you also expect that over time, that Investment Asset will go up in value (appreciate). When it has gone up in value enough for you to be willing to sell the Asset, the difference between what you paid for the Asset and the price you sell the Asset for, is called the capital gain. This gain is taxable income to you and must be reported on your tax return in the year you sold the asset.

Alimony and Child Support. (Passive Income) When you receive money as part of a settlement of divorce, the money designated by the courts as alimony and child support is considered income to you because it is money that flows into your possession. Any money you must pay out as alimony or child support is considered an expense for your purposes.

For tax purposes, Alimony is usually considered taxable income which you must include on your tax return. Any money you receive as child support usually does not need to be reported on your tax return, it is not considered taxable income. (Check your State's laws and the Divorce documents to know of any adjustments that you need to consider.) The person paying the Alimony can deduct the alimony paid as a reduction to their income on their tax return, but they cannot deduct the cost of child support from their taxable income.

Business Income (Usually Active Income) from a sole proprietor business or farm. If you engage in some form of business, whether it is a hobby or a real desire to earn money, the net income, the gross income minus the expenses of the hobby or business, is considered income to the owner of the business. Many times, a small business owner will think they are making a lot of money because they consider the gross income as their income when their real income from the business is just the net income (total income minus total expenses). Do not make the mistake of many small business owners by spending the income before you pay the expenses. This habit, while tempting, will only leave you with a declining business.

Income from Trusts or Partnerships (Usually Passive Income unless you are a partner that works for the company). Some people receive money from trusts or partnerships, this is a type of business income and again the net income is the amount you truly receive, not the gross income that passes into the company. If you spend the gross and forget to pay the expenses of the business, the business will soon have to close the doors to the business. Net business income is taxable income to the recipient and must be reported on the tax return.

Rental Income. (Passive Income) When you own something and rent it out to another person for their use, usually property, the net income after expenses is considered income to the owner of the property.

Whether you buy land and wait for it to appreciate in value or you buy property to rent out, you will receive some form of ROI, either the net rent or the capital gain. These incomes are taxable and need to be reported on the tax return.

Royalty Income. (Passive Income) When you write a book and people buy the book from you or the company selling your book, you receive royalties. Those royalties minus any expenses you incur while you are writing the book or marketing the book are considered income to the author. I call this Passive Income even though you might have put in the hours to write the book, once it is published, your "work" is done. You are not being paid by the hour to sell the book; you just receive the money when the book sells.

Unemployment Income. (Passive Income) This income is received when you are no longer employed, and you file with the State for income to get you through until you find your next job. This is considered income to the receiver and is taxable. Keep in mind, that most people think this income is tax free, but it is not and seldom does the issuing organization withhold the needed taxes. You must come up with that money when you file your tax return.

Other Income. (Could be either Passive or Active) There are a variety of other ways to receive income that are not related to your work or business. This could include gambling winnings, contract earnings as an independent contractor, jury duty pay, pay as the executor of an estate, and a whole lot more.

Retirement Income. (Passive Income) This comes from monies you or your employer put into accounts that will provide income for you after you stop working. Most of these accounts incur a penalty if you take the money out before you are 59 ½ years of age. These include pensions, IRAs, Roth IRAs, Annuities, 401ks, 403bs, and 457 accounts.

Social Security payouts to you when you retire will be considered retirement income. You will never know how much income is generated by your Social Security until you have finished your tax return for a given year. I say this because Social Security payouts are taxed based upon how much other income you have in retirement. Some people with low income do not have to pay income tax on their Social Security payouts. Others, who have additional areas of income in retirement can have up to 85% of the Social Security payout be taxable income.

Insurance Benefits, Inheritance Distributions, and Worker's Comp and Disability Income. (Passive Income) These benefits come to you as income even though most of them are not taxable income. These payouts usually come to you because something has happened to you or to someone you love. You could be the beneficiary of an insurance policy that pays you when someone gets hurt or dies. A relative could die and leave you part of their estate. In all these cases, you will receive income. Some of it might be taxable; most is not.

Sources of "Income" that are Not included in the Income category.

When you borrow money from someone, either a friend, family member, or even a bank, you have a perceived source of Income; the money does flow in so you can spend it. But it is not Income, it becomes for you, a Liability; something you must pay back at some point. Whether it is a short-term loan to get you through a difficult time or a long-term loan to purchase an Asset, you need to be aware of the Liability you are creating for yourself when you borrow money. It will need to be paid back.

This is true for Credit Cards as well. Credit cards allow you to borrow from the "bank" and spend their money. In return you give them the permission to charge you a rate of interest on the balance of that loan until you pay it back.

This feels like income because you can spend it on any expense you want but, you are creating an obligation which you must pay back at some point and it usually carries with it an interest charge. Try to avoid any form of loan that carries with it a high interest rate; by high I mean anything over 10%.

The actual income from liabilities that appear to be income is often minimal. If however, you have the opportunity to borrow money to invest in an Asset and the net income of the Asset is greater than the expense to pay it back, you might have created an Income Generator that will benefit you in the future.

Active Income vs Passive Income

There are two major categories of Income as I have mentioned; Active Income and Passive Income.

Active Income is income that you do have to work for, you do have to show up to work, and you need to spend your time and effort to actively pursue your income. If you are not at work, you do not get paid. This happens to many small business owners who do not have the benefits of being paid when sick, or taking time off, enjoying holidays, etc.

Passive Income is income that you did not have to work for, that is not dependent upon you showing up to work, that is not based upon the time you spend at the job. It is income where your money or investment is working for you. It could be a franchise you own but do not actively manage because you have someone you trust doing that for you. Or, it could be your investments that are growing in value while you are involved in your work or just enjoying your life.

It is a reasonable goal to arrive at some point in your life where your passive income is greater than your active income. You do not ever have to stop working if you do not want to, but with a growing amount of passive income coming your way, you give yourself the freedom to choose if you want to work and if so, what you want to do.

Work should be fun and rewarding. Strive to make your active income a job you enjoy and can excel at, so you have enough to set aside and someday enjoy the blessings of passive income as well.

Chapter Four;

Expenses, Spending Money

The Profit & Loss Statement	The Balance Sheet
Active Income: Work Passive Income: Savings	Income Generators Non-Income Generators
Necessary Expenses Optional Expenses	Liabilities: money you owe Liabilities: money you borrow to make money

Remember the Richest Man in Babylon? He took 9 coins out of his pocket for every 10 he put in. Spending less that you earn is the single most important lesson you will ever learn. And if you practice it, you will be financially blessed the rest of your life. What you do with the tenth coin will be talked about later in the book, but used rightly, you will have a storehouse of wealth from which you can do almost anything you desire.

There are two major categories of Expenses; Necessary and Optional. The necessary are a combination of requirements for living and self-imposed obligations. You need a place to live, food to eat, and clothing to wear. As you get older you might also need transportation, insurance, healthcare costs, and the like.

Self-imposed obligations come from your choices. When you choose to buy something, you cannot afford you obligate yourself for the future. Now you have a loan you are obligated to pay back in a required amount of time at a certain interest rate. Or because of some purchase you now have the responsibility and the cost to maintain the product you chose to buy. This is not an obligation imposed on you by life or by someone else, it is something you imposed upon yourself. Just remember when you are going to purchase something you cannot afford; it always takes longer to pay off the loan or costs more to maintain than you would have expected when you entered into the agreement. Paying off the loan also takes longer than waiting until you have saved up enough to buy the item outright.

Once your necessities are paid and you have satisfied your self-imposed obligations, you might have additional options. If you have set aside your 1 coin and spent some of your 9 coins on necessities and self-imposed obligations, you have options as to how you will spend any coins you have left over. These options or extras will include nicer clothing, going out to eat, various kinds of entertainment, and the like.

It is very important to remember that options become obligations when you borrow money. Too many self-imposed obligations added to your necessities will begin to limit the amount of money you have available to spend on optional activities.

The Two Big Expenses

I like to think of these two expenses as something you take care of before you begin to look at how many coins you have "Put in Your Pocket." For instance, you bring home your paycheck in $1 bills and lay them out on the counter in your house. You could consider all that money as your 10 coins and begin by setting aside your 1 coin from all those dollar bills. But the "big two" expenses seem to be the most important expenses you will ever pay out. So, what if you took the big two away from all the $1 bills and then thought of the amount you had left as the 10 coins you have to work with?

As an example, your gross paycheck is $100. You come home and layout the 100 one-dollar bills. You could put 10 bills in your savings and put the other 90 bills in your "pocket" to spend. Or you could take the needed money to cover the big two away, say 20 one-dollar-bills and work with the 80 you have left over. Then 8 bills get set aside in savings as the 1 coin and the nine coins is the 72 one-dollar bills left to spend.

Hopefully, you get the idea. I realize, you never bring home the $100 from your paycheck since taxes are taken out before you get home. And those taxes are the first of the Big Two expenses that everyone has to think about.

Taxes, the first of the Big Two.

The Big Two Expenses are Taxes and Charity. Most people have some taxes taken out of their paycheck before they bring it home. That is a good thing for all of us. Because almost everyone I know has trouble saving money. If they also had to save for their taxes, they would never have enough money to pay the taxes when they are due.

Some self-employed people need to set their tax money aside by Estimating how much tax they might owe and pay that amount into the IRS on a quarterly basis. These are called Estimated Taxes. If you are self-employed and you do not pay enough Estimated Taxes during the year you might have to pay a penalty at the time you file your Income Tax Return.

No one knows how much they will owe in taxes at the end of the year. You might get a refund, or you might have to pay more when you file your return. Either way, you will not know how much total tax you paid until you complete your filing.

A word about the refund you might get from your tax filing. If the refund is large, it does not mean the government is giving you money. A large refund means you let the government use your money during the year without interest. You loaned them money and they did not pay you any return.

The amount you must pay in taxes is based upon your income and deductions. Whether the money is taken out of your paycheck throughout the year or you must pay taxes with your return, you still must pay the same amount in taxes. What you owe is what you owe; how you choose to pay the tax is your choice. You can change your w-4 form at work to have the company take out more or less tax from every paycheck. That is your choice, but you will have to settle up with the IRS at the end of year on your tax return. If you get a refund, you paid them too much during the year. If you must pay, you did not pay them enough during the year.

Charity, second of the Big Two.

Why give to charity and why is it something to do before you calculate your savings? Charities give you the opportunity to be generous with your money and help other people. I think of it as a personal welfare program. When I buy cookies from the Girl Scouts or raffle tickets for the school fund raiser, I am giving from my resources to meet the needs of others. When I give to the church or some other non-profit organization, I have the opportunity to give generously. The United Way is a local group of charities who meet the needs of many people in our communities. There are so many charities around us that would appreciate our gift that we can never give to them all.

But let me encourage you to think about it this way. Giving is not just about what it can do for the organization or the people the organization serves but giving also brings great benefit to the giver. You become a better person when you give.

If we take everything we have and spend it on ourselves, we become more and more selfish. Selfishness can turn into greed if it is not controlled. And a person who lives with a growing amount of greed in their lives will soon find nothing good in their lives. The greatest cure for greed and selfishness is to give some of your resources away to help others in their need. It is very hard to be greedy and generous at the same time.

Giving often starts by little gifts. A small gesture toward helping others will grow on you over time. I do not want to scare you but the more you give, the more you want to give. However, only give if you want to. Try it and see if you don't like it.

But you might be wondering how giving and then giving more, benefits you because it seems that it is just taking your money away from you.

The interesting thing a person learns on this journey toward generosity is the more you give away to help others the more you have left to give away. It seems logical that if you give something away you have less, but with generosity it does not work that way. It is a spiritual teaching of Jesus, but I think it is a spiritual principle that God ingrained into the fabric of life. The more you give away, the further what you have left, will go.

Generosity and greed are opposites and when you cultivate generosity in your life, you receive an equal or greater benefit in return. Just because you give someone $100 today does not mean you will find a $100 check in your mailbox tomorrow. But the more you give away, the more you get in return; whether it is money, kindness, love, etc. And you do not feel the loss, you feel the gain. Spiritually, it is a greater blessing to give than to get. It is also true, spiritually speaking, that the way you treat others is the way they will treat you.

Setting aside the One Coin. Saving.

Now that you have taken the Big Two expenses out of your total income, you are left with your ten coins. What do you do next? You only take 9 coins out of your pocket. Even though the story of the Richest Man in Babylon says you only take nine out, the one-coins you leave in your pocket will soon get too heavy to carry around.

So, let's change the plan. For every 10 coins you put in your pocket, take the first one out and save it. Then spend the rest.

Learning early in your life to set aside money from every paycheck is the best way to accumulate Income Generators for your future. I will talk about what to do with the savings later in the book, just start setting it aside now. Do not touch it until it is making money for you.

By way of reminder, it does not take a lot of money at each moment to build a large amount of money over time. $5 a day generates almost $2,000 per year. And $2,000 per year generates $80,000 over 40 years without adding interest, and $100,000 in 50 years. If you could invest that $2,000 per year at 5% annual interest, you would have $241,600 in your account after 40 years and $ 418,700 in 50 years. And that is just $5 per day at 5% annual interest.

At the writing of this book, my grandson Marcus, was 19 years old and I was 72. That was a 53 year difference. If he started saving a little each day, or week, or month, by the time he would be 72 he would amass a large amount of money. Investing $5 per day at 5% interest for those 53 years returns the sum of $517,000; over a half a million dollars. What if you put $6 a day or received 6% interest?

Spending the 9 coins.

You now have a chance to spend the 9 coins you have left. What are you going to spend them on? Let's split your expenses into two categories; Necessary Expenses and Optional Expenses.

Necessary Expenses are house, food, clothing, and maybe transportation. Optional Expenses include everything else. If you are comfortable hanging around the house all the time, buy a big luxurious house and sit back and enjoy. If you want to get out and explore the world you will need to buy or rent a smaller house in a less expensive part of the world so you can have lots of extra cash left over to go do your exploring.

Just keep in mind, every time you use your 9 coins to buy something that needs ongoing maintenance, or you borrow coins from someone else to buy something you can't afford right now, you are obligating yourself for the future. Once you are strapped with an ongoing obligation you increase your Necessary Expenses and reduce your available coins for the extras you want in life.

A Thought About Quality.

When you are thinking about purchasing something, ask yourself a few questions.

How long / often will I need this? If I will not need it often or for a long time, consider renting it or buying something with a little less quality and cost that will last long enough for your need.

Can I rent it? People have many things lying around their homes which they used only once. They could have rented it for a fee and given it back when they were done. Almost anything that is not disposable is rentable. And if you rent it you know it is the latest model and in working condition.

Think about the economics of movies, something I like to watch: a movie in the theatre costs $10 now. Renting the DVD from a movie store costs $3 a time. Buying a subscription to Netflix or some other service costs less than $20 per month for all the movies you want to watch. Based on the number of times you watch a movie in a month, which is the best option for you. Or does your cable company offer movies for free?

Can I buy a better quality? If the purchase you are thinking about will be something you will own and use for years to come, consider spending a little more up front and buying a better quality. Often people shop based on price alone and that works fine for things you might not want to keep for a long time. If you plan to keep the item for a long period of time or use it often you might choose to do some research and purchase quality for the long run.

Cars can be purchased or leased. Leased is less expensive on a monthly basis, but at the end of the lease you either must lease another car or buy the leased car. If you end up buying the leased car, you would have been better off financially buying the car in the first place. However, if you like the joy of driving a newer car every three years, and you can afford it, by all means, lease and enjoy. If you own a small business you might be able to write off the cost of the lease and reduce your Net Income.

Lowering Expenses.

When your financial picture gets out of control, and it does for most people, there are a few tricks to bring things back under control.

You can reduce your spending.

What are things you can do without? One less cup of coffee, one less meal out, one less cigarette, one less movie, one less trip in the car, and so on. Remember every $5 per day you do not spend, and you save could be $250,000 in 40 years. Remember to put the saved $5 in the savings.

You could borrow your books from the library, put off purchases until they go on sale, shop at the thrift stores in your community, and make a variety of other changes to reduce your expenses. And whenever possible, wait 30 days before you purchase anything; you often will find you do not need the item anyway.

On big expenses like rent or buying houses and cars you can always settle for a little less space, or a bit older car. Just do your homework so that paying less now does not become higher maintenance fees later. A friend of mine always drove older cars, kept them well maintained, and put a nice radio system in the car. It did not matter to him what the car looked like, just that it ran well, and he could enjoy the music.

Some simple tricks to save money daily include; always shopping with a list, plan your menus when you are hungry but only shop after you have eaten, and make one trip with several errands rather than multiple trips.

You may be thinking you have bigger problems and these types of tips will not make a dent in your budget issues, but a multitude of these small tips practiced over a long time will make major changes in your habits. Those major changes will over time cause you to make better decisions. Better decisions will change your life for years to come.

Avoid, as much as possible, credit card debt of any kind, debt consolidation schemes, and refinancing loans to absorb other debts. And when you do have loans and credit card debt, pay more than the monthly minimum and stop adding to the loan. Oh, and stop borrowing in the first place.

Recycling, Reusing.

A great way to lower expenses comes in the form of reusing things or buying at thrift stores. Far too often I have gone to the store to buy something new and I look back on all the times I could have just gone to the thrift store or a garage sale and found what I was looking for. And a lot less expensive.

"One man's trash is another man's treasure." Or so the saying goes. And if you go to the goodwill or other thrift store, they might even recondition something before they put it in the store for sale. And then you end up with almost new for dirt cheap prices.

Chapter Five:

Assets, the things of value you own.

The Profit & Loss Statement	The Balance Sheet
Active Income: Work Passive Income: Savings	Income Generators Non-Income Generators
Necessary Expenses Optional Expenses	Liabilities: money you owe Liabilities: money you borrow to make money

Assets come in two categories; those that ***do generate income*** along with their value, and those that ***do not generate income*** but have some value. It is that simple. A house you purchase to rent out to others does generate income if the income is more than the expenses of the mortgage, taxes, and utilities, etc. A house you live in does not generate income, but it has financial value.

Some examples of Assets that do generate income include houses you rent out to others, savings accounts, business Assets, investment accounts, etc. Assets that do not generate income include houses to live in, automobiles unless they are appreciating in value, jewelry, and other collectables.

Why do you need to understand this distinction? To highlight to you the need to accumulate Assets that generate some income for you rather than purchasing Assets that will just increase your expenses. Now, houses to live in are not a bad choice, but they can be if not understood properly. I want you to understand the different kinds of Assets you can own.

Kinds of Assets:

Real Property. Primary Residence.

Many people think the purchase of a personal residence is a valuable Asset. It has "income generating" type value when the mortgage is paid off and your expenses go down accordingly. It also has value when you sell the property for a profit, i.e., more than you paid for it and put into it over the years. It becomes a non-producing property when you refinance it and take the value out of the house; you exchange your equity or value for a debt that you owe, an obligation. Unless you use that "equity" to purchase an income generating Asset, you have turned your potentially good Asset into a financially draining Liability.

When I lived in central California, I wanted to purchase a house. I had owned a house in Minnesota and sold the house for more money than I paid for it. I thought that would always happen if you bought a house. Well, not always. My friends in the central valley owned their own home and it did not go up in value at all in the seven years I lived next door to them. That meant, I could have bought a home when I moved to town and sold it seven years later. I would have lost money because I would have had to pay the real estate commission of 6% on the sale price. Not a gain at all.

When I moved to costal California, I bought a house and over the next 15 years it doubled in value. I tried to sell it and it would not sell. So, I waited another two years and it doubled again. I sold it for four times what I paid for it. You never know what will happen with the value of property.

Just a thought, renting can often be a better option for you than purchasing. While your rent is not going towards something that will increase in value, you also do not have to fix every problem in the house, faucets, roofs, water heaters, etc. You can just call the property owner, and have it fixed. This reduces your expenses on an ongoing basis. Many people think that owning is the way to go but they forget the fact they have repairs on the house. Before you buy, consider the history of asset appreciation in your community.

Real Property. Rental Property.

If you can afford to purchase a property and rent it out to others, you might have an income generator. You wonder why I say, might. The rule of thumb I have been guided by is this: if the rent you charge for 10 months is more than the cost of the mortgage, taxes, insurance, repairs and any other costs you might have to pay; then the property is generating income. If this formula works for you, then you make even more money if you rent the property out 12 months of the year. Keep in mind, if you do not rent the house out for the full 10 months, you might lose money; be prepared to pay the costs during the down time.

The benefit of owning rental property for a long period of time is similar to the time value of money. Rents usually go up over time and your income increases. Your expenses do go up but often not as much as the rents go up. Most rental mortgages are 15 years rather than 30, so at the end of 15 years you own the property outright and your income goes up the amount of the mortgage payment you have been paying. And, over the long-term the value of your property usually increases with the rise in property values in the area. Now, you end up with a piece of property free from debt, a low property tax level, minimal expenses and much higher rents. Win-win for you the landowner.

Automobiles and Trucks.

When can a vehicle be an income producing Asset? When it is appreciating in value or when it is used for business.

If you buy a classic car and the value is going up, you might have an investment; but you need to know when to sell it and be willing to do so when that time comes. Investing in autos for profit means you must stay in touch with the market and sell when the value is high. Often these values go up and down based upon the number of people wanting the type and model of car you own.

If you buy a vehicle you can use for business; like using a truck for hauling junk for a fee or driving your car for some rideshare program for a fee; you can make money from this Asset. However, like in rental property, you should consider purchasing a vehicle for business only if the income from the business outweighs all the expenses. I have worked with a lot of people over the years who believe their business is making money because they have money coming in, cash flow. They forget to consider how much money needs to be spent to generate the income. Many times, I find they are not making any money or not enough to make it worth their while in the long run.

Otherwise, your vehicle might be fun to drive, but it will probably not generate any income for you. It is an Asset with depreciating value. Thus, it is not an income-producing Asset.

So, if vehicles do not go up in value and usually do not generate income, should you own a vehicle? Maybe, maybe not. Most new cars cost you at least $500 per month to own (purchase, insurance, gas, repairs, etc.). You can lease a car for less. You might not need a car except for certain occasions, so you might rent one when needed, or call a rideshare. You must be the one who decides what is the best way for you to get around to the places you go. And you need to weigh the costs with the convenience so you can make a wise decision on owning a vehicle. Can you ride the bus and get where you need to go?

Remember that new vehicles normally do not need a lot of maintenance costs, but they decrease in value almost 20% in the first year. After 4 years most cars are worth less than ½ their original value.

Be sure to check out maintenance records of certain makes of cars and buy something that is at least 2 years old with a good service record rather than paying full price for a new car that will lose a lot of value in the first two years you own the car.

Business Assets.

Assets that can be used to engage in business might help you generate income. Businesses do not always generate income. Read chapter 16 on Starting a Business before you make that leap.

However, one of the best ways to increase your Income Generator is to own a business and especially a business that does not depend on your hourly rate of return. If you offer people a service in your business and you are the one performing the service, you will be getting paid by the hour. Even if you can charge $100 per hour you can only make $200,000 per year unless you work yourself to death. And that $200,000 is not all yours. You will need to pay taxes on the money, pay expenses of the business from the money, and the only way you can make $200,000 is working 40 billable hours every week, all year long. More later.

Investment Accounts.

These accounts are where you invest your money in some form of Stock or Fixed Income strategy and it hopefully provides you some sort of income in its gain in value. At first you might not need the income and so you will reinvest your income and let the investment increase in value. But someday you would like this investment account to generate regular income for you, so you no longer have to "go to work."

There are two types of investment accounts and they both have their own value: Taxable accounts and Retirement (tax-deferred) Accounts.

Taxable accounts mean that all the income generated by the investments in these accounts may be taxed in the year it was paid out. Interest and dividends will be taxed for sure, however gain in value of a stock or other security may not be taxed until it is sold. Those are the three ways an investment account generates "income." Even if you reinvest your gains, you will have to pay the appropriate taxes. Interest is taxed as if it was additional wages you earned. Most dividends are taxed at a special rate depending on your Adjusted Gross Income; it might be 0%; or 15%; or even 20%.

Capital Gains happen when an investment is sold. The difference between what you paid for an item and the sale price of the item is the Capital Gain. The Capital Gains tax rate is the same as the rates for Dividends. If you never sell the individual stock, you can defer the tax on the capital gains because that tax is only calculated and paid in the year of the sale of the stock.

There is an exception to this information if you own the stock for less than a full year. Short-term Capital Gains are taxed as regular income and you will pay the same percentage on these gains you pay on your income.

A Mutual Fund is a bit different. When you purchase shares in a Mutual Fund you might receive Capital Gains distributions at some point during the year. These will be reported to you on a form 1099 Div. The mutual fund manager passes on to the shareholders the current net capital gains or losses, both short term and long term, for the investments inside the mutual fund. Those capital gains or losses which are attributable to your shares of the fund will be reported to you and you will need to claim them on your tax return for the year. Keep in mind that you might have to pay tax on Mutual Fund Capital Gains even though you did not actually have the dividends and gains paid out to you.

Tax deferred accounts (retirement accounts) mean that you do not pay tax on the interest, dividends, or capital gains until you take the money out of the account. In this way, all the income generated by the investment is not taxed as you go but is tax deferred. You will usually pay taxes based on your current income tax rate when you withdraw money from the account. Keep in mind, these accounts have a lot of regulations on them and you cannot easily get your money out of the account without paying a penalty unless you are over 59 ½ years of age.

Collectibles and Other Valuables.

You may or may not list your Jewelry or Stamp Collection on your Balance Sheet as an Asset but in fact anything that you purchase with a plan to resell at a higher price could be considered an Asset.

There are some wines that go up in value every year and you might know enough to purchase them now, hold them for a few years and sell them later for a profit. This income would be reported on your tax return as a capital gain in most cases. These wines are an Asset that will generate income for you in the future. In lieu of selling the wine at the higher rate, you could donate the wine to a local charity auction and receive the full amount as a charitable donation. This will benefit you if you are able to file a Schedule A on your tax return.

Other wines that you put in your wine cellar so that it will taste better in a few years and you drink it, will never generate income for you, but you will have an increased amount of pleasure from that Asset.

Chapter Six:

Liabilities

The Profit & Loss Statement	The Balance Sheet
Active Income: Work Passive Income: Savings	Income Generators Non-Income Generators
Necessary Expenses Optional Expenses	Normal Liabilities Helpful Liabilities

From time to time people choose to borrow money to purchase something they feel they need to have right away. They do not have enough money to make the purchase. So, they borrow money from someone, make the purchase, and then pay off the loan later. This loan is a Liability.

The loan can come from the bank directly as a loan or from a bank indirectly in the form of a credit card. In either case, what you owe is a Liability you have. You cannot ignore your liabilities; they will need to be paid at some point. Some people have avoided their liabilities by going bankrupt, but that is an extreme case and it would be better not to accumulate too many liabilities in the first place.

There are two categories of liabilities; I call them Normal and Helpful. Normal liabilities are the ones most people have while Helpful liabilities are those that are helping you generate income.

Normal Liabilities.

Mortgages on your house, car loans, and credit card debt are the normal loans people have in their Liability section of the personal Balance Sheet. You might even list the loans you received from individuals, like parents, as liabilities because you should expect to pay them back at some time.

While these liabilities allow you to purchase things now and pay them off later, they normally do not generate income for you, they often just increase your "necessary" expenses over time. When your expenses increase unnecessarily, your net income (revenue minus expenses) goes down and you have less money to put into income generating investments.

In business, the liabilities include unpaid wages and taxes, unpaid invoices from suppliers, etc. Many times, a business will save up money to be paid out later, sometimes in just a few days. These monies are said to be accruing until the time they are paid out. These accrued monies are liabilities because they will need to be paid out.

Helpful Liabilities.

Distinct from normal liabilities, helpful liabilities refer to their ability to help you generate income. If you go into debt so that you can make money off the corresponding Asset, you might consider this Liability as a helpful or good one.

A helpful Liability would be when your business borrows money for equipment or other property that you will use to generate your business' income. If the loan is seen as an additional expense and the business can still make a profit at the end of the period, the loan (Liability) has been helpful for your business and enabled you to make a greater profit.

On a personal note: a helpful Liability would be the loan associated with the purchase of a rental property which you have figured will make money for you. This loan will be paid back with the rents on a monthly basis. Again, as I said earlier, make sure your rent for 10 months is enough to pay the expenses, otherwise you will be using your own money to buy the property and it is no longer making you money. If the property is not making you money, the loan against the property will fall back into the Normal Liability category.

Goals in Life.

When strategizing about your liabilities you will want to think in terms of reducing your normal liabilities and increasing your helpful liabilities. If the money you owe has a purpose and its own income-generating Asset, the Liability has a good, helpful purpose.

Chapter Seven:

Taxes, paying the government.

The Profit & Loss Statement	The Balance Sheet
Active Income: Work Passive Income: Savings	Income Generators Non-Income Generators
Necessary Expenses Taxes Optional Expenses	Normal Liabilities Helpful Liabilities

Earlier in the book, I mentioned the Two Big Expenses. Taxes was the first one. Before you can begin to look at your money and decide how many coins you will have left to work with, Taxes will need to be paid.

Income Taxes are usually deducted from your paycheck and you only see the money as part of the gross paycheck, but never as the amount you take home. This is also true of Social Security and Medicare taxes which also are paycheck deductions.

Jesus spoke to His disciples about paying taxes, "Pay to the then king of Rome, Caesar, the things that are Caesar's and to God the things that belong to Him." A wise proverb says, "the only two things guaranteed in life are death and taxes." Taxes are an inevitable part of our life. But there are some benefits to taxes.

Benefits to Paying Taxes.

First, if you owe taxes, it means you made some money. Granted, in the United States' system, the more money you make the higher percentage rate you pay in taxes, but you never have to pay 100% of your income in taxes. The highest current income tax rate (2019) is 37% for married couples who make over 600,000 adjusted gross income (500,000 for singles). That means for every dollar over $600,000 after deductions, you must pay 37 cents of it to the government for income taxes.

Second, you get to live in a great country. With all our faults, as a country, most people in this world would love to live here. Many people seek to move here every year.

Third, our government pays for our country's welfare system. Without the country's welfare system, taking care of the poor and needy would be dealt with by churches, local communities and non-profits. They would be asking you for a lot more money and more often if the Federal Government and most State governments did not pay for a lot of our welfare programs out of the tax money. However, keep in mind, that most government welfare programs are more expensive than local programs because of the greater need for oversight and the higher potential for corruption.

Fourth, taxes cover the cost of First Responders; Police, Fire, Sheriffs, Highway Patrol, as well as our prison systems, etc. Without these professionals, many of these services would be provided by local volunteers or not provided at all.

Fifth, taxes pay for education costs for all Americans. From kindergarten through college, taxes provide some amount of the basic costs, if not all the costs of public education. And it is true, an educated populace makes for a better country in every situation.

Sixth, without taxes, our roads and bridges, sewers, water system, and in general, our infrastructure would be haphazardly repaired. We would not know what to expect on roads and bridges from county to county.

Seventh, some of the cost of healthcare is provided through our tax structure as our welfare programs include emergency services to the poor and needy.

We might not like to pay taxes, but the costs of these services would be significantly higher if we were called upon to provide these services in our local community without the help of State and Federal governments.

Taxes We Pay.

Payroll Taxes

Income Tax, both the Federal government and most State governments impose upon you a tax related to the amount of money you make in your job. States that do not impose tax on your income receive their revenue through some other form of taxation.

Social Security and Medicare Tax is charged by the Federal government in the form of a payroll deduction of 7.65%, which is matched by your employer. Self-employed persons are required to pay both their own share and their employer's (self) share of this tax. This tax covers the costs of the Social Security System, retirement income, disability income, certain death benefits, and the Medicare System, basic healthcare costs for the elderly and some others.

Non-Payroll Taxes

Sales Tax, most States and local governments collect a certain amount of tax on many of your purchases. Again, if your state does not collect a sales tax, they probably charge a higher rate in either Income Tax or Property Tax. Taxation is the major source of revenue for government agencies.

Subtle Tax, I just made that name up because it occurs to me, we pay taxes in the form of fees all the time. When the government entity doesn't think the public would vote for an increase in taxes, they get around it by imposing a fee rather than a tax. In truth, the fees are another form of taxes we all pay.

Property Tax is paid by people who own real property. It is usually a percentage of the assessed value of the property. In most cases the County Assessor's office sets a value for each piece of property and taxes are paid on that amount. The value set by the assessor usually has nothing to do with how much a piece of property is worth if a person tried to sell it. So, there are two definitions of property value, the assessed value for tax purposes and the sale value if you wish to sell your property.

The sale value of property is subject to the Real Estate market. The market is set by the number of houses available to sell and the number of buyers who are interested in purchasing houses. This is called the law of supply and demand. If the supply is low and the demand is high, the value of the house goes up because there are so many people wanting to purchase a house. If the supply is high and the demand is low, the value of the house goes down.

For instance, more people wish to move to the coast of California than those who wish to move to some small town in the middle of Nebraska. Consequently, the value of property on the coast of California is usually much greater than the value of property in the small towns of Nebraska.

Capital Gains Tax, when a person purchases something of value; property, stock, collectables, etc.

the cost they pay for the item is what is called the "cost basis." Then when they sell the item, the difference between the net sales price and the cost basis is called the Capital Gain, and the seller will need to pay a tax on the gain. This is usually done at the time of filing a tax return where the individual is required to list the gain on their tax return and pay the appropriate tax.

Other Taxes, there are various other places where governments choose to impose taxes on people; personal property, business property, gas taxes, entertainment taxes, and the like.

Chapter Eight;

Charity, the benefits of giving away.

The Profit & Loss Statement	The Balance Sheet
Active Income: Work Passive Income: Savings	Income Generators Non-Income Generators
Necessary Expenses Taxes Charity Optional Expenses	Normal Liabilities Helpful Liabilities

I have called this the second of the Big Two expenses. I call it a necessary part of your expenses because of the great value it is to you to give money away. I will speak more about that in the next few pages.

The amount you pay in Payroll Taxes and the amount you give in Charitable Gifts combined are, in my way of thinking, not considered a part of your 10 coins you put in your pocket. These two expenses are so critical to both the country you live in and the quality of life you live, that I have always thought of them as coming out of my money first, before I start to divide up my savings and other expenses.

The Benefits of Giving Away Some of your Wealth

Being charitable or generous, giving some of your money away to others, has a variety of benefits to you and to the society where you live:

First, a good non-profit to whom you would give the money is **meeting the needs of someone in this world who has less** than you have. By giving to the non-profit you are providing someone a job and you are sharing in the work they do of meeting the needs of others.

Second, one of the goals of giving is to overcome greed. The more you give away, the more **you loosen the grip of greed in your life**. Giving expands your horizons beyond yourself. Greed on the other hand causes you to become more and more selfish. You cannot remain stagnant, you will either loosen up your attitude and life by giving or tighten up your attitudes and life and ultimately ruin it, by being greedy.

Third, giving gives back to you. Whether you talk about good karma or you believe in Jesus' teaching, the more you give to others the more others give to you. What goes around comes around. How you treat others will be how they treat you. You might not notice it right away, but over time you will see the benefit of being generous towards others with money, with time, and even, with attitude.

Fourth, science now has concluded that **if you are generous in your attitude you will live longer**. Good things come your way when you are generous and treat people fairly. (Psalm 112 verse 5)

Fifth, it has also been tested and found to be true that **people who are generous in their lives are happier** than those who grudgingly keep things to themselves.

Sixth, just for fun, there is something I have found over the years, **the more I desire to protect what I have and try to grow my savings, the more I watch it slip away.** It just does not have the value it should have if I am greedy or stingy. The Book of Proverbs, in the Bible, says the more you want to hold on to what you have, the less you have because you will have "holes in your pockets" and "your money will slip through your fingers." These are not literal holes in your pockets but you spend more money or things come your way that force you to spend money and you soon find out you have quite a bit less than you thought you should have.

Principles of Giving

The way you give to others should be the way you want others to give to you. Treat others how you wish to be treated. That is one of Jesus' teachings and is often called The Golden Rule. "Do unto others as you would have them do unto you." This is just a good spiritual principle in life.

I do not think you can give too much, and I am not just talking about money. However, I had a friend in Minnesota who gave away money and things while forgetting that his own family needed money and things at home. So, you can give away more than you have available, especially if you have other people depending upon you.

Someone once asked whether you should give a percentage based on your gross income (before taxes) or net income (after taxes). The answer is this: "Do you want a gross blessing (big) or a net blessing (smaller) in return?" Your return will be proportional to your giving.

Make giving a habit. Start small; give a little away. But do it again in a short amount of time. And just learn to give regularly. It doesn't have to be to the same place, but it could be. The goal is to give, and then give some more. Make it a habit.

Give before you determine the value of your ten coins. If you pay your payroll taxes and set aside the money you will be giving away, then you can call what is left as the 10 coins you have that are yours to work with.

On a spiritual note: *Love of material things and spiritual growth are mutually exclusive. The more you love this world and the things in it, the less chance you have of developing your spirituality. That does not mean that rich people cannot be spiritual, but it is much more* *difficult. At the same time, if a person cannot be competent with the material world, i.e. money and possessions, and manage them well, they will have difficulty managing their spiritual life also.*

Avenues of Giving

Non-profit organizations are formed by people interested in helping those in need. If you can find an organization that resonates with your passions check out their information. If most of your giving to them will end up helping others, by all means, find ways to support the organization with your time and your giving. Every good organization does need some structure and management. A rule of thumb is 10-20% of the overall expenses of the organization can go to administration. But you would like most of your gift to go to the work of the organization.

Please do your research as many non-profits spend quite a bit more on administration than on the work they do. They purchase property and buildings rather than do the service to others that they claim to be doing. They might pay their staff enormous wages and very little trickles down to the cause they say they support.

Churches provide another opportunity for you to give of your time and resources to help other people. While churches often spend much of their money on the salaries for staff and expenses for the facility, they often do the majority of their work through the staff and the facility. They usually do not charge for their programs or services either.

People doing good works can also be an opportunity for you to give to meet the needs of others. You might know someone who is doing something good for the community but does not have a corporation or non-profit they work through. Even though you might not get a tax deduction for your gift, the goal is not to make tax deductible donations but to give of your resources to meet the needs of others less fortunate than you. If you get a tax deduction, that is an added benefit.

Friends can provide you another opportunity to share your resources with others who have a need. There may be times that your friends need a little extra in their life and you have something to offer them. There may well come a time in your life when you will be in need and a friend will help you out.

Tax Deductions

Whether a gift is tax deductible or not should not rank as a high priority in choosing where you do your giving. Two things you should know about tax deductions:

First, you may not get to deduct your giving anyway since the Government has raised the Standard Deduction for single and married filers making it more difficult to qualify for a deduction.

Second, even if your contribution can qualify as a deduction, you do not get all of your money back in your tax filing. If you give a $1,000 contribution to a non-profit and claim it as a deduction on your taxes, you will reduce your taxable income by that $1,000 but you will only reduce your taxes owed by the amount of your tax bracket. If you are in the 10% tax bracket, you will pay $100 less in taxes than you would have otherwise when you give $1,000. If you are in the 25% tax bracket you will pay $250 less in taxes for your $1000 contribution. Either way, your gift to the non-profit still cost you $900 in the first example and $750 in the second. If your contribution benefits you with a tax deduction, that's great, but the larger benefit comes to you because you have given something away.

Find ways to give to others, take what you have and pass it on to someone else; either a person or an organization you believe in. If it happens to be tax deductible, fine. But that should not be your goal. Your goal in giving is to free yourself up from greed and selfishness. People who are greedy and selfish do not live happy lives. Those who are generous and caring for others live happy lives even when they spend a lot of time serving others.

This Page Intentionally Left Blank

Chapter Nine;

Saving Money

Top

The Profit & Loss Statement	The Balance Sheet
Active Income: Work Passive Income: Savings	Income Generators Savings/Investment Non-Income Generators
Necessary Expenses Taxes Charity Optional Expenses	Normal Liabilities Helpful Liabilities

Remember, for every ten coins you put in your pocket, only take out nine. After you have paid your tax obligation and your choice of giving to others, you have a certain amount of money left over. Out of these

“10 coins” left over, learn to only spend nine of the coins and save the other 1.

What does it mean to save?

Saving has many definitions Are you saving for a specific purchase you have your heart set on? Are you just putting money in a savings account because you do not have anything to do with it yet? Are you saving for a “rainy day?” Are you setting money aside for later? Or, are you thinking ahead and getting ready for retirement?

The idea of the Richest Man in Babylon is simple. Take one of every ten coins and do not spend it. Ever. That means saving for a future purpose does not qualify as saving, it is just postponing an expense for a later time.

The tenth coin would serve you best if it was put in an investment that will someday generate income for the rest of your life.

There are four levels of Savings Accounts.

Reserve Account.

A prudent way to handle your finances is to build a savings account that equals about three months’ worth of your budget. If you spend $6,000 per month on your expenses, then the reserve account should have $18,000 in value. This reserve is ready if you become unemployed or have a serious accident or an unexpected expense that is greater than your cash flow can handle at that moment.

If you need to pull money from the reserve account for an emergency expense, remember, your first task would be to replenish the reserve account to its full three months value. So, take all the money you allocate to savings, your one coin from the next paychecks, and build your reserve account back up to its needed value.

Over time the reserve account will need to increase in value since your spending habits will change; you might get a raise and can now spend more or the cost of living will go up and you choose to spend more. When you are spending $7,000 per month your reserve account needs to increase to $21,000.

Reserve account money should be invested in an account where the money is easy to get to when it is needed. You would not expect to receive a high rate of interest on this account. Your goal in this account is not to gain money but to preserve it and have it available when needed.

Project Funds.

As I mentioned earlier, a project fund is just a delayed expense. You are setting money aside so that it can build up in value until you have the amount you need to purchase what you want. This fund should be money that is part of the 9 coins because it is just a delayed expense not really a 1-coin savings account. The 1 coin left in your pocket needs to be placed somewhere that generates a long-term investment not a delayed expenditure.

Retirement Accounts.

These accounts can be tax-deferred, non-taxed, or taxable accounts. This is money you are setting aside to draw on in the future when you no longer have a steady flow of income from work. These accounts should be seen as Income Generators. You can choose from three types of accounts; Tax-deferred, Non-taxed, and Taxable.

Tax-deferred accounts

The traditional retirement accounts are 401k, IRA, ANNUITIES, SEP, SIMPLE, 403b, and 457 plans. The government designed these accounts to allow an investor to accumulate their capital gains and interest/dividends over a longer period of time and not pay taxes until the money is withdrawn from the account; thus deferring paying the taxes. The plans restrict the outflow of money until a person reaches the age of 59 ½. Then when a person reaches the age of 70 ½ they must start taking a distribution annually.

One of the great benefits of the tax deferred account is this: the amount of money you put into the account can be deducted from your taxable income in the tax year you make the deposit. You can make the deposit any time during a tax year; from January 1st of the year, until the date you actually file your taxes; which could be as late as October 15th of the following year. You can determine with your tax advisor how much to put into your retirement account and how much you will benefit from the reduced income you report.

Most tax deferred accounts have limits as to how much money you can put into the account each year. Even if you are putting only $5,000 per year into an IRA, you can accumulate $200,000 in the account without even collecting interest or gains after 40 years. With an interest rate of 5% you have amassed over $600,000; three times what you put in. In 50 years, those numbers are $250,000 and $1,000,000 respectively; that is over 4 times the money you put into the account. Remember the lesson of the time value of money. And the government increases the amount you can put into the accounts on a regular basis.

When you put the money into these retirement accounts, any investment growth, interest and dividends you receive is not taxed on an annual basis. It will be taxed when you take the money out of the account. If you take the money out before you are 59 ½ you will be charged a 10% penalty, with some exceptions. Anytime you withdraw money from these accounts the amount will be added to your taxable income, and you will pay income tax on the money at your current tax rate.

The institution that holds your tax deferred accounts will send you a 1099 R form at the end of each year you withdraw money from the account, so you can include this information in your tax return. Usually, the 1099 R will indicate the need for the money to be claimed as taxable income.

If you are transferring money from one tax deferred account to another, that might be indicated on the 1099 R, if the transfer is within the same institution. If the transfer is not within the same institution, you will not receive any form that tells the IRS you have deposited the money back into another tax-deferred account. You will just have to state that on your return in the proper place. Money that is taken out of a tax deferred retirement account and then returned to the same account or another tax-deferred retirement account within 6 months is not included in taxable income. However, if the 6 months has lapsed, the distribution will be considered taxable income.

A Word about Annuities

Annuities are tax-deferred retirement accounts that come out of the insurance industry and often combine a type of life insurance as well as a tax-deferred investment account. They have many of the same constraints you will find in all retirement accounts about withdrawals. The accounts can let you invest in stocks or bonds or just be a savings account. You should read the fine print on the contract before you get yourself locked into an annuity. They had a bad history of enticing investors to deposit money and then making them pay penalties to withdraw the money early even when they wanted to just move the money from one tax deferred account to another.

Usually, the annuity does not have a limit on how much you can deposit each year, unless the annuity is an investment inside of another retirement account. In this case, which I do not encourage you to do, you are investing in a tax-deferred annuity, inside of a tax-deferred account. You only benefit once from a tax-deferred vehicle.

Non-taxed accounts

In the late 1990s the Federal Government created a ROTH IRA account. The ROTH is a non-taxed retirement account. The money you put into the account has been taxed already, so you get no income deduction for putting money into the account. When you take money out of the account you receive the money tax free.

The institution that holds your ROTH account will send you a 1099 R, just like all the other retirement accounts, but the box 7 coding will indicate that the distribution does not need to be included in your taxable income.

Another variation on a non-taxed retirement account is something the Federal Government set up in 2015, allowing a person who is 70 ½ to give money out of their IRA account directly to a qualifying charity and not have to pay taxes on the money "withdrawn." You cannot claim the deduction on your Schedule A, but you will not have to claim the withdrawal as income either. If you are a person who likes to give, and as I suggested earlier, I think you should become such a person, then this will be a great way to legally avoid paying taxes in the future. For example; you want to give a non-profit organization a gift of $500 per month for the year. Rather than writing a check out of your checking account, you could have your investment company send the $6,000 directly to the charity. And the distribution also qualifies as a part of your RMD. It is a win-win.

A Word about Beneficiaries

All tax deferred and non-taxed retirement accounts ask you to designate a beneficiary. You need to choose a person or persons you wish to have benefit from your investment if and when you die. Whatever money is left in the account when you die will be sent to the listed beneficiaries.

It is important to review your choice of beneficiary from time to time. I have seen often where the person who dies never changed their beneficiary and people who they no longer like, end up with all their inheritance rather than the people they want to have it. For instance, a man divorces his wife and does not want her to receive anything from his will or trust at the time of his death. But he forgets to change the beneficiary designation on his retirement account, and she gets the bulk of his estate because of his oversight.

Taxable Retirement Accounts

You can also put money in a regular investment account to save for the future (retirement) without having the account be tax deferred. In this case you will be paying taxes on your interest, dividends, and capital gains in the year they are realized. Even so, you still are putting money aside for retirement and you have no limits on how much you can put in or when you can take your money out.

Taxable Retirement Accounts are just investment accounts that you choose to invest in to grow your portfolio for your future benefit.

Strategic Retirement Investing

I recommend to people they invest for retirement using the following strategic use of the various accounts:

1. If your company offers you a match on your money you put into a 401k or 403b type account, take advantage of your employer's generosity first. They might match up to 3% of your salary, or one dollar for every two you invest up to 4% of your salary. Whatever they offer try to do the maximum amount to take advantage of the "free" money before you do any other kind of retirement savings.
2. Once you have reached the limit of the employer's match to your money, then take any additional amount you have chosen to save for retirement and invest it into a ROTH up to the limit that the IRS will allow for you during that year. This will give you the best return for the future because it will be tax free distributions.
3. If you still have money left over after you put the maximum allowable into your ROTH, then go back to your 401k type account and max out your contributions.
4. When you have accomplished all of this and still have money to save for the future, put the money into a taxable retirement account.

The Goal of Retirement Investing

The point of the retirement account is to build Income Generators while you are working so you will have a source of income when you stop working. The age you choose to stop working and start drawing income from your accounts depends on your choices. If you have enough income being generated from your investments so that you do not have to work, you might choose to stop working. The longer you work, the more money you can save from your paycheck and the less you will have to draw on your investments. That just allows the investments to generate more income that you reinvest until you need to draw on your investments to use for actual living expenses.

When I say, draw on your investments, I mean you will be able to withdraw between 4% and 5% of the value of your investments in any given year. If you just draw 4% of your money and the money is not gaining any interest or growth, your money will last you 25 years. (i.e. 100% of your money divided by 4% is 25) If your investment is growing your money will last much longer than 25 years by withdrawing only 4%.

Income Generators.

Any Income Generator fits into this category of savings. It could be a taxable account, an annuity, a whole life insurance policy, a small business, or even investing in collectibles, the goal is to continue growing your ability to produce Income without you having to work for it. Then you will be free to retire whenever you choose and spend your time doing the things you love to do.

The real key to an Income Generator is to have your money working for you, generating a return of Passive Income. What can you do with your money to Generate Income? Well, that will take us into the next chapter where we talk about investments. But for now, just realize that your goal for all your savings accounts is to Generate Income now and in the future.

Whether you invest inside of retirement accounts or buy a business you are seeking to use your "savings" to Generate Income for yourself. Few people make an investment of some form, hoping to lose money; they usually want to gain a return on their investment.

As you will see in the next chapter; the greater the return you hope to receive is dependent upon the amount of risk you are willing to take. Those people who do not want to lose their money, their principle, are low risk investors and do not often purchase a business or invest in stocks. Those who are willing to take a risk move into more risky investments like stocks or businesses. I will talk more about this in the next chapter on Investing.

Learning to Save.

Saving money is not easy for most people; it is an art form that is learned over time. Having a goal, what you want to accomplish, helps a lot in the process.

You might be reading this and be thinking that you are already behind, your expenses are more than the nine coins, you are in debt, and there is no way you can begin saving. But you can learn to save.

The first step in learning to save is changing your thinking. You just need to begin to put the ten coins principle into practice as much as you possibly can. Maybe you can only put 1 coin in savings for every 100 coins you put in your pocket. Begin there. Accept the importance of saving and expect that you will put something aside out of every paycheck.

The second step is the doing. Get yourself a "Money Jar." Set it on your bedroom dresser, or the fireplace mantle or the middle of the living room table or in front of the TV. Every time you see the jar, put some money in it. Coins, bills, or whatever you have. When the jar starts to get full, take it to the bank and open a savings account. And then put the jar back in its prominent place and start filling it up again.

Some employers will let you set up a direct deposit from your paycheck to go to a savings account. Have a small amount withdrawn from your paycheck and put into the savings. You do not have to put in a lot, you just have to start putting money in. When you think about it and can afford it, ask your employer to take a little more out. Every time you receive a raise, start putting a little more aside.

I have a change jar in my house. I put change in it every time I come home. Twice a year I cash it in and put the $150 to good use. If I didn't already have my savings accounts set up, I would be putting that change into an account that would "work" for me. As it is, I use it to make another contribution to my favorite charity.

Saving $5-dollar bills is another way to begin saving. Every time you have a $5-dollar bill in your pocket pull it out and put it in your "money jar." I did this one time and 6 months later I counted $400 worth of $5-dollar bills.

There are hundreds of ways you can save $5 dollars at a time.

1. Skip a meal once a week.
2. Skip Starbucks and go to McDonalds for your coffee.
3. Stop drinking alcohol at one meal per week.
4. Smoke less cigarettes.
5. Get Netflix and quit going to the Theatre.
6. Choose to eat only salad at one meal per week; the dinner salad, no meat.
7. Avoid afternoon treats.
8. Take the bus rather than drive your own car; your car costs you 54 cents a mile to drive.
9. Pay down your credit card bill so your minimum payment is $5 less each month.
10. Buy your next purchase on sale.
11. Have a list when you shop and do not buy extra things.
12. Rent something rather than buy it.
13. Buy Generic.
14. Avoid convenience stores.
15. Purchase in quantity.

Pick one and begin to practice saving. Saving is something that starts as a small discipline and becomes over time a challenge and even a joy. When you become faithful with your discipline, you will begin to get excited about what you have accumulated and what you can do. You will not want to stop. And each time you put money in the Jar, you will be putting in a little more. You will start going to the bank more often to put your savings to work for you.

Every time you skip a meal or buy less expensive coffee or make some other choice that will save you money, put the money you saved into the Money Jar. Watch your saving grow.

You will not only be saving you will be growing in your confidence in yourself. You can be creative. You can find ways to forgo something that you think you cannot live without and put the money in the Money Jar.

Begin saving, do not stop saving, and watch your savings grow.

Chapter Ten:

Investing

Top

The Profit & Loss Statement	The Balance Sheet
Active Income: Work Passive Income: Savings	Income Generators Savings/Investment Non-Income Generators
Necessary Expenses Taxes Charity Optional Expenses	Normal Liabilities Helpful Liabilities

Investing, by definition, is taking your money and "giving it to someone else" in exchange for them returning your money to you (maybe) and with some amount of interest. You are loaning your money out to others and they are paying you some return for the privilege of using your money for a period.

Whether you put the money in the bank or give it to someone else or buy a business, you are setting your money aside, investing with the hopes of receiving more in return.

Many times, you put your money into an account at a financial institution and inside of that account you purchase certain types of investments. Depending upon your willingness to risk your money, you will seek to gain differing amounts of interest or return. Some of the accounts you choose will determine if you are investing for a short time or for a long time. And over time you will develop a strategy for your investing that will work best for you, your willingness to risk, and the return on investment you would like to achieve.

In this chapter we want to offer a brief review of the types of accounts, investments, risk, and strategies available to you as you start to invest your money. Then I will list for you some of the basic principles of investing that will help you understand the nature of investments.

Types of Accounts

Some of this information was covered in the chapter on Retirement savings but it will be helpful to review it in this context as well.

Tax-deferred Accounts

Tax deferred accounts come in the form of retirement accounts (401k, 403b, 457, IRAs, and Annuities). When you leave the money in the account, the taxes on interest, dividends, and capital gains will be deferred until you withdraw money from the account. After you reach the age of 70 ½ you will have to withdraw a percentage of money every year; this is known as the Required Minimum Distribution (RMD).

The benefit of most tax deferred accounts comes in the form of a tax deduction in the year the money is put into the account. This allows you to put the money in, get the tax break now, and then wait until you withdraw the money before you will need to pay taxes; hence the term tax deferred.

Within these accounts you can invest in a variety of investments and no matter the return on your money, you do not pay any taxes until you take the money out. When you take the money out, called withdrawing money or taking a distribution, you will add this money to your income on your tax return and pay appropriate taxes on that amount.

The real benefit of these accounts is allowing your return on investment to grow and receive interest on your interest without having to pay the taxes in the year you receive the return. You have no tax consequences when you sell investments within the account and buy other investments because the account is a tax deferred account.

The original selling point of the tax deferred accounts was your changing tax bracket. When you are working, so the theory went, you would be in a higher tax bracket than when you retired. That has not always been the case. Even so, most tax deferred accounts have proven to be a good way to invest over a long period of time.

Tax Free Accounts

The only way I know of to invest your money and not have to pay income tax in the year you receive the interest, dividend or capital gain is to use a ROTH IRA. These accounts encourage people to pay tax on all their income in the year they earned it.

In a ROTH account you deposit money that has already had the income taxes paid. So, you are placing after tax dollars into the account. Then as the investment gains over time, you can take the money out and not have to pay taxes on the distribution. There is no required distribution (RMD) from a ROTH after 70 ½. You can keep the money in the ROTH for as long as you desire.

One catch, you can only put money into the account if you have wages in the year you make the deposit. And you can only put as much money into the ROTH as you have wages, up to the limit set by the government. For example, if you go to work when you are 80 years old and make $1,000, you can put all of it in the ROTH account. If you make $10,000, you can put in the maximum amount the government allows. If you do not make any wages, but you have lots of other income you cannot put anything into a ROTH account.

Taxable Accounts

Most bank and brokerage accounts are considered Taxable accounts. You will have to pay your income taxes in the year you earn the interest, dividend or capital gain. You must claim those events on your tax return. The institution will send you a 1099 Div. form at the end of each year to let you know the amount and type of income you will need to report on your income tax filing.

Capital gains come when you sell an investment that you have previously purchased. The difference between the sale price and the purchase price is the amount of the capital gain or loss. The institution reports the information you need to you on the form 1099 during the month of January of the next year. On your tax return you will be asked to provide the date you purchased the investment, the date you sold it, the price you paid (the cost basis), and the price you sold it for.

Broker Assisted, Advised Accounts

Broker advised accounts mean you hire a broker or brokerage firm to assist you in making choices for investments within the accounts you own. You will pay a fee of some sort, but you will have the help of a professional advisor as you manage your money in the account.

Some financial gurus make a big point about not paying brokerage fees because the fees "lower" your investment returns. However, it would be best to talk with your broker and determine if your net return is better one way or the other; i.e. total return paying no fees with one firm vs total return minus the broker fees with the other firm. Many people find the assistance of the broker to be worth the amount you agree to pay him or her. You make the call.

I have often found that the broker is so helpful that the net return is higher with their help than when I try to do things on my own.

Not only do I need to consider the return of my investment, I should also consider the time involved in choosing the investments. The question will often boil down to how much I believe my time is worth and how willing I am to become adequately informed about investments and the overall trends of the economy.

Self-Advised Accounts

Self-advised accounts are those account where you open the account, usually online, and without any assistance from a broker, choose your investments. You might save a few percentage points on the fees, but do you save enough to compensate yourself for the time and effort you put it to making investment decisions. Most people do not make wise money-making decisions without the help of the seasoned professional.

Types of Investments

Once you understand the types of accounts available, you need some education on the type of investments you will want to use. These usually fall into six general categories; Cash, Fixed Income (Bonds), Stocks, Mutual Funds, Real Estate, and Small Businesses.

Cash is more than just a roll of dollar bills stuffed under your mattress. The category of cash includes bank accounts, savings accounts, and money market accounts. Cash investments are usually available right away. You do not have to sell something or wait a few days for the bank to give you your money. It is as available as the cash in your wallet.

Fixed Income defines investments where you put your money with an entity, and they promise to pay you a fixed amount of interest over a longer period. To get money out of these investments you either must wait until the date of maturity or you pay a penalty to get your money out of the investment before the date of maturity.

The category of fixed income includes CDs, saving bonds, treasuries, government bonds, municipal bonds, and corporate bonds.

CDs come from your banking institutions and have a fixed amount of interest for a fixed number of months or years. Government treasuries and bonds, likewise, have the fixed interest and timeline and are issued to the people by the federal government. You can purchase them through most brokers or sometimes directly from the US Government.

Municipal bonds are issued for various projects in the State, Counties, and Cities. If they issue a bond to build a school or repair a road, it is usually called a General Obligation bond. The interest the municipality pays you comes out of their general budget. When the municipality chooses to build something, they expect to make money from like a toll bridge or road, they will issue a Revenue bond. The interest the municipality pays you comes out of the revenue generated by the tolls or fees people pay to use the project.

With a Corporate bond you are loaning your money directly to the corporation and the corporation agrees to pay you a fixed interest rate for a fixed period. This interest comes from their general budget and is considered an expense to the corporation.

All Bond investments have a fixed rate of interest paid to you over a set period of time; i.e. 4% interest and the bond matures 5 years from the date of issue. The interest rate will vary from Bond to Bond based upon the date it is issued and the date the Bond matures; i.e. when they will pay you back the money you loaned to them. In the meantime, you will receive interest payments on a regular basis.

Stocks refer to shares of stock in the actual company. If you own 100 shares of a company that has 1000 total shares; you own 10% of the company. Owning stock in a specific company authorizes you to attend the shareholder's meetings, vote at the election for the board of directors, and carry out other privileges of partial owners of the company.

When you buy the shares of stock from the brokerage company or on the stock exchange, you are not paying money to the company. Once the company has sold their initial offering of stock to the public, all future transactions of stock, buys and sells, are transactions between the current owner of the shares and the new owner of the shares. The company is not involved at all except to change the records of who currently owns those shares.

When you own the stock, your shares will go up and down in value depending on the number of people who want to buy the stock or want to sell the stock. Most of the buyers and sellers are influenced by the profits and projections of the company as reported in their quarterly earnings report. This information is readily available for any publicly traded company.

Mutual Funds and Exchange Traded Funds (ETFs) are not really a type of investment but are a collection of types of investments managed by a person or company with a clearly defined goal in mind. The Fund might invest in a wide variety of stocks or bonds or they might invest in a specific sector of stocks, i.e. just technology companies. The Fund must, by law, print a prospectus of how they plan to manage the Fund and publish that prospectus. Any person wishing to purchase shares in a Mutual Fund or ETF must receive a copy of the prospectus when they offer to buy shares in the Fund. The management of the Fund must adhere to their plan as printed in the prospectus. If they choose to do something different than what is stated in the prospectus, they must notify their investors and give them time to sell their shares and invest somewhere else.

A Mutual Fund or ETF is not a different investment vehicle from a Stock or Fixed Income or Cash; it is a vehicle that gathers Stocks, Fixed Income (Bonds) and Cash into one group, under one management group, and markets their Fund according to the rules of the specific Stock Exchange.

Mutual Funds and ETFs are often labeled based on the size of companies and the kind of companies they invest in. You will notice that the size and kind is often listed in the title of the Fund; Large Cap Growth Fund; International Small Cap; Growth and Income, etc. The definitions of some of the common size and kind nomenclature will be listed later in this chapter.

Real Estate investing is another form of getting your money out there with the hopes of a return in the future. Whereas stocks can be sold and the money available to you in three days, real estate requires a longer period to get your cash out of the investment.

That being said, real estate can be a great investment. Purchasing a home, although it is an Asset on your balance sheet, does not generate for you any income per say. It does reduce your expenses, but unless you rent out the rooms to someone else you do not receive income.

In some locations, investing in vacant land can also be an "income" generator. One way you make money on just land is to rent it out to someone who wants to farm on the land you own, and they will pay you rent to use the land. Another way would be to own the land long enough for it to appreciate in value and you make the income on the land when you sell the land for more than you paid for it.

Most real estate investments include rental income; either residential or commercial. Both types of investments require some effort on your part but can generate for you a net income after expenses are paid.

A good rule of thumb for rental real estate investing says that you should only purchase property that will generate a profit for you if it is only rented 10 months of the year. That profit does not need to be more than $1 but it needs to be a profit. The expenses involved in rental property include; mortgage, property taxes, insurance, utilities, repairs, property management, bookkeeping and tax reporting, and appropriate legal fees. After all of these are paid and some incidental other costs, if you make a slight profit you will be on your way to generating income from your Real Estate investment.

At first, with Real Estate the amount of income in not as important as the fact that there is some income. Over time, the rents in the locale will go up and you will have an increasing source of income. Also, if you hold the property long enough, the mortgage will be paid off and your income for the property will increase even more because your major expense of mortgage no longer needs to be paid each month.

Small Business investing is another way for you to put your money out with the hopes of receiving interest in return. I have included chapter sixteen to give you some ideas about going into business for yourself. Most small businesses fail within the first couple of years and often a person signs a three-year lease, so they still have the lease to pay without the income from the business. Those who choose the right business for them and run it well can find a small business to be a great investment.

Cryptocurrencies are a relatively new form of investing. Some would call it gambling. These investments are highly volatile and risky. As mentioned earlier, when trying to get an ROI greater than the current market average (right now, about 10%) you are also taking a greater risk of losing everything you have invested. If you follow the ideas behind diversification, which will be talked about in a few pages, you would never put more than 5% of your overall portfolio in Cryptocurrencies. At the same time, many seasoned investors do invest in Crypto.

Types of Risk

I have shared with you about types of accounts for your "savings" and the types of investments you can use in those accounts to generate ongoing income for yourself. The next area of discussion related to investments has to do with your tolerance for how much money you are willing to lose in order to gain money.

All investments except low interest cash accounts will include some potential of fluctuating value. The amount of money you place in the investment can go up and down in value. The amount of that fluctuation depends on the risk level of the investment.

Risk is often categorized in three different levels; conservative, moderate, and aggressive. This is a continuum with conservative being one extreme and

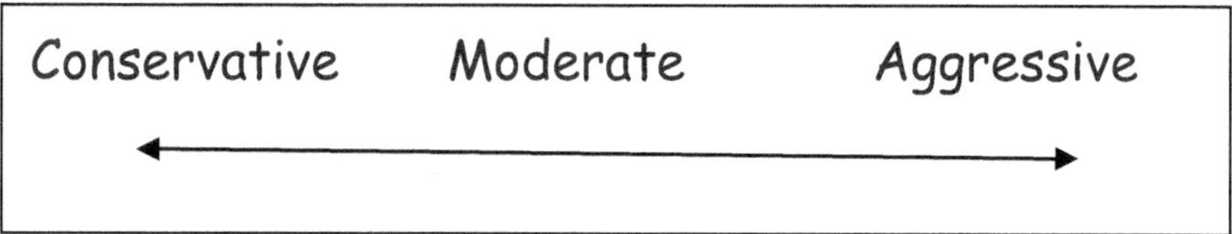

aggressive on the complete other end and moderate fits in the middle. Like this:

As you can see, there are many places along the continuum you can find yourself when you define your own risk tolerance. You might think of yourself as somewhere between moderate and aggressive or maybe you are very close to conservative. There is no right place to be on the continuum, it just depends on where you feel comfortable.

Conservative means you want some return, but you do not want your money (your principle amount) to ever go down in value. Aggressive means you are willing to watch the value of your money fluctuate with the hopes of seeing some higher rate of return in the long run.

A conservative investor might never put their money anyplace other than a bank savings account where they earn a modest amount of interest. They are happy seeing the statement at the end of the month showing that their money is still in the account and they have gained a small amount of interest.

An aggressive investor might put all their money in very volatile company's stock hoping that the value of the stock will go up over time faster than most other investments. They are willing to see their "principle" be significantly lower when they see the monthly statement because they expect, in time, the stock will go back up to a much higher value than when they originally purchased it.

The moderate investor finds a place on the continuum line somewhere between Conservative and Aggressive where they feel most comfortable. Your investment broker can help you determine which investments are right for you and your personal risk tolerance.

There is no right Risk level for all people. Each person needs to determine how much they are willing to risk in order to generate an income from their monies. Usually, the amount of return you desire from your investment is determined by the amount of Risk you are willing to take with your money. The more conservative risk level investments generate the lowest amount of returns. On the other hand, the most aggressive risk level investments can, but do not always, generate the higher rate of return.

Types of Strategies

Basic Account Investment Strategies

If you have money to invest, whether it is because of excess income, inheritance, or winning the lottery, here is the order of investing that I recommend for the best use of your money. And remember, you do not begin investing until you have set money aside into your Reserve Account, which is the account you will use for emergencies and should have the equivalent of three months-worth of your average expenses.

After you have set aside your reserve account begin your investing by putting money into your 401k or similar plan at work up to the amount your employer will match your contributions. Then place your next available amounts of money into your ROTH IRA until you have contributed the maximum allowable for the year.

If you have a spouse, contribute to their ROTH IRA up to the limit set by the IRS provided they have earned income to that amount. Contributions to ROTH IRAs must "come from" wages or earned income.

You can then add money to your 401k type accounts up to the maximum allowable by the IRS.

If you still have money to invest/save, then you can put the money into a taxable account. Based upon your total investment portfolio, all your accounts, spread your investments out according to the type of account:

401k type accounts should contain your most conservative to moderate fixed income and stock investments because they will be taxed when you withdraw the money later in life.

ROTH IRA accounts should contain your most aggressive investments because your hope is, they will grow the fastest and the most. Because the ROTH allows you to withdraw money from the account tax free under most scenarios, you will pay less taxes on the growth of your investments in this account.

Taxable accounts should contain your most conservative investments that pay interest and dividends during the year but do not distribute capital gains until you choose to sell the investment. Remember, mutual funds buy and sell stocks and bonds within the mutual fund during the year. Then at year's end they send you a 1099 form indicating your share of the capital gains distributions for the year. You are required to include those capital gain distributions on your income taxes whether they have paid you the money or not. Usually they "pay" you these gains in share value, not in cash. You might have to come up with the money to pay the taxes. That is why you want your mutual funds to be included in tax free or tax deferred accounts.

Percentage of Stocks vs Bonds.

Depending on your risk tolerance as talked about before, you might want to reconsider the percentage of stocks in your total investments. An extremely conservative level of stocks in a portfolio is close to 0%; meaning you would have 100% in Cash and Fixed Income.

The only risk a super conservative investor is making is Interest Rate Risk. Even though most interest rates on investments are fixed at the time you invest that interest rate might not keep up with inflation. If the interest rate you are receiving is not more than the current rate of inflation you will lose buying power with your money. Your actual dollars will still be in the account but the amount of goods they can buy will decrease as time goes on.

A super aggressive investor might go to the level of 100% in stocks and 0% in bonds. You are willing to risk all your money because you believe that even though the stock market goes up and down, it has historically provided investors an average of 8% per year return.

Most people will be somewhere in the moderate or middle range of risk and investing.

The rule of thumb for most money managers of large trust funds, or other investment portfolios would be somewhere between 40% to 75% of the total investments in stock. The younger you are the easier it would be for you to build your portfolio back up if you lost a lot. The older you are, especially when you are retired, you do not have the earning power to go out and rebuild your portfolio if a major loss occurred. Consequently, most older people become a bit more conservative as they age.

For the New Investor

As you begin your investing, I would suggest you put your money equally into three Mutual Funds within a retirement account. One of those funds should be a Growth Stock Fund, one an Income Stock Fund, and the third a Bond Fund. These will be explained in the next few pages.

However, begin your investing with this strategy until you learn about the stock market. Look at the market daily. Watch how and why it goes up and down. Maybe even try a few trades on paper; write down what you "bought" and then what you "sold" and see if you are making money.

After about three months look at your original three investments and rebalance your account to make them all equal again; sell some of the fund that has grown the most and put it in the fund that has not grown much at all.

Any new money you put into your savings, invest equally into the three different funds. In this way, you are seeking to maintain an investment portfolio that is 66% stock and 34% fixed income.

Keep working on your learning about the markets. Try all your "hunches" on paper, not with real money. If you are right most of the time, you might begin to put real money into your investments, but remember, speculate or gamble with no more than 5% of your total portfolio at any one time. You will have plenty of time to become more aggressive and take more risk with your money as you grow in your wisdom about investing.

Start now, with an auto deduction from your bank account every month. And do not stop. Always increase the amount being deducted, do not decrease it. Keep adding to your three funds until you have over $ 100,000 invested. Then begin to branch out.

10 Definitions You Need to Know

The Market Maker

When a company sells their stock to the public, often called an initial public offering (IPO) they receive money and the buyers receive shares of the company's stock. From that point on the company is out of the mix. They do not sell stock, nor do they receive more money, unless they have a secondary offering of stock. When you buy shares of stock you buy it from someone like you who already owns the stock; they sell to you and you pay them. This process of buying and selling is handled by the Stock Markets; New York Stock Exchange, and the Nasdaq.

Inside these Exchanges or "Markets" there are people who facilitate this buying and selling. You tell your broker or online company what you want to do. They contact the person inside the Market or Exchange who trades the company's stock you wish to buy. And that person makes your trade happen. This person is called the Market Maker.

The Market Maker determines the price of the stock based upon the number of shares people say they want to buy, and the number of shares people say they are willing to sell. On the New York Stock Exchange there is only one Market Maker for any one company's stock. That person continually monitors the buyers and the sellers and negotiates the trades that people want to make. The Market Maker makes a small amount of money on every transaction.

The Market Maker has many rules and regulations to follow in order to fairly set the prices of the stocks being traded on the market.

What Makes the Markets go Up and Down?

The simple answer to why the stock market fluctuates has to do with buying and selling. If today, more people want to buy stock than sell stock, the demand is higher than the supply of shares, and the market, i.e. the price of the stock, will go up. If on the other hand, more people want to sell their shares than people want to buy those shares the price must become lower so the buyers will purchase the stock. The Market Maker assesses this information on a minute by minute basis and changes the prices as needed to sell more shares to the buyers and entice the sellers to sell.

Principle of supply and demand.

A general principle of the capitalistic system which we use in the United States and functions at the heart of the stock market is the principle of supply and demand.

If you have 10 apples and 20 people want one apple, you can sell each apple for more money than if you had 10 apples and only 5 people wanted an apple. Your supply has not changed, but the demand has. You have to lower your price to entice people to buy your apples.

Shares of Stock on the Stock Exchanges change hands at a price "set by the market." That means "set by the demand on those shares." If 100 people each own 100 shares of a company's stock the price will go up and down based on who wants to buy and who wants to sell. If lots of people would be willing to sell their stock at a higher price, then the value of the shares might go up, until the buyers say they do not wish to pay that price.

A market left to itself will usually set a "fair" price based upon this principle. Other influences can get in the way of a "fair" price. In the stock market, the exchanges set rules by which the Market Makers must abide in order to have fair trading of stocks and bonds.

Expectations.

When you are considering an investment, you should be aware of your own personal expectations. Regardless of what an investment has done in the past you cannot predict what that same investment will do in the future. If someone suggests to you that an investment will make more than the going rate of interest in the financial world, you might want to be cautious.

While the Stock Market has historically grown at a rate of around 8% annual return, you do not know if next year will be up 26% or down 26%. An annual return of 8% means that over time, the average rate of return is around 8% per year. If you keep adjusting your investments every time you become spooked by the news about the markets, and you sell your stocks and then buy them back a day or two later, you will not necessarily make the average 8%.

Remember, if someone tries to sell you an investment that pays much more than 10% per year in return, you should check things out in great detail before you give that person your money to invest.

Diversification.

Diversification is a term used in investing that keeps you from putting "all of your eggs in one basket." If you total up all the money you have in your investments, you want to be sure that you do not have more than 5% of your total portfolio invested in any one company. You want to be diversified or have your investments spread out.

Keep in mind, a mutual fund is made up of a lot of stocks. The 5% rule does not apply to mutual funds, but to the underlying stocks inside them. If I own 4% of my portfolio in Apple Stock and I own a mutual fund that invests in Apple; I need to make sure that mutual funds position in Apple is less than 1% of my portfolio. If I own many mutual funds and they all have a holding in Apple stock, I might not wish to own the Apple stock outright. I might sell it because I am not well diversified at that point.

Diversification needs to be tested across sectors as well. There are times when people think technology is the greatest investment, and many technology stocks have done exceptionally well, but to have over 5% of your investment money in technology related stocks can be very risky. At the time of the Tech Bubble in the year 2000, the NASDAQ index, which is largely technology related stocks was trading around

5000 points. In the course of a few months the NASDAQ was trading very near 2000. A drop of 60%.

What do you think you would have felt like if you lost 60% of your whole portfolio in a few short months? Twenty years later the NASDAQ is back to 5000 but some of the well-loved stocks of the late 1990s are no longer a part of the NASDAQ index.

Company Sizes; Micro, Small, Midsized, Large

There are four arbitrary valuations of company size. They are called micro, small, midsized, and large. The size of a company is based on their Capitalization. Capitalization refers to the multiple of the number of outstanding shares of the company and the price of the shares on a given day.

An example: Apple Corp, has close to 20 billion shares outstanding, or owned by investors. The company has sold that many shares to the public. Today, as I write this, Apple is trading at an all-time high of $151 per share. That means the market capitalization of Apple at this moment is almost 3 trillion dollars.

Microcap means the company has less than 250 million dollars of Capitalization. So, Smile Direct Club, as of today, is a Microcap company.

Small Cap refers to companies with a Capitalization between 250 million and 1 billion dollars,

Mid Cap companies have between 1 billion and 5 billion dollars in Capitalization, while

Large Cap companies have over 5 billion dollars in Capitalization.

Growth or Income Stocks.

Growth Stocks refer to companies that pay little or no dividend back to their shareholders because they are in growth mode. They are reinvesting their income back into various aspects of the growth of the company.

Income Stocks refer to companies that pay a dividend back to the shareholders from the profits of the company. Many of these companies have left behind the phase of growing the business and are now looking at ways to improve or expand different areas of the company. Since they do not always need their large amounts of cash to make purchases of other companies, they can give some of the money to their shareholders in the form of a dividend.

Bonds and other Cash type investments can be considered as Income investments because they pay a regular interest or dividend. These investments are often found in both Growth and Income Mutual Funds in small quantities while the manager is looking to buy more stocks.

When a mutual fund claims to be a Growth and Income Fund they usually invest in Stocks, some growth stocks and some income stocks. If a Mutual Fund wishes to invest in Stocks and Bonds the title of the fund usually is considered a Balanced fund.

Sectors is a term used to refer to stocks in different categories based upon the product or services the companies provide; Building materials, Technology, Financial Services, Industrials, Healthcare, Utilities, Energy, etc. Mutual Funds and Exchange Traded Funds are often categorized according to these sectors allowing investors to invest an amount of money in one sector.

Foreign, International Stocks/Funds.

While the definition of these terms is not the same to every person, usually, these terms are not interchangeable. I define Foreign Funds as funds that invest in companies based outside the United States. On the other hand, I see International funds investing in companies based outside the United States and companies based inside the United States.

Interest Rate vs Inflation

I mentioned this idea earlier but for emphasis I will bring it up one more time. The rate of inflation is a measurement as to how much a certain economy is growing. The United States economy usually grows in the 2% to 3% range every year. This economic growth is measured and reported on a quarterly basis. It defines approximately how much more it costs this year than last year to have the same type of lifestyle.

If the rate of return you receive from your investments is less that the rate of inflation, the buying power of your money will diminish. Even though you have more money in your account, you can buy less with that amount of money because the money cannot purchase as much as it could last year. Prices have gone up but the value of the buying power of the money has gone down.

In most cases, you want your investment portfolio to be growing faster than the rate of inflation. If your investments grow at a rate of 3% but the inflation rate is 4% then you are losing ground. If the growth rate is 3% and the inflation is 2% then you are 1% ahead. It is important to design your total investment portfolio so that you exceed the rate of inflation on a regular basis, especially if you plan to use the return on your investments as income in the future.

Chapter Eleven:

Budgeting your Money

The Profit & Loss Statement	The Balance Sheet
Active Income: Work Passive Income: Savings	Income Generators Savings/Investment Non-Income Generators
Necessary Expenses Taxes Charity Optional Expenses	Normal Liabilities Helpful Liabilities

Any discussion about finances must include something about budgeting. A Budget for your money involves planning out the costs of living your life over the coming year, or some other period. This is a good time to look at your expenses as we talked back in Chapter 4. How many of your expenses are in the

Necessary category and how many are in the Optional category.

A Budget fits the Profit and Loss Statement. What are your sources of income and your estimates of that revenue? What do you estimate your taxes to be and how much money do you plan to give away? At this point you can determine the value of the 1 coin that you will add to your savings during the year, either at work in your 401k plan or through one of the other investment accounts and tools. Then divide up the 9 coins into your needed amounts for your Necessary Expenses and your Optional Spending. This exercise will help you plan out your year and make the needed adjustments along the way when certain expenses are more or less than you planned.

In the old days, back when I was starting out, you could buy a "wallet" at the stationary store to help. This wallet had a leather cover and it included about 15-20 envelopes. You could write on the envelopes the different expenses you were budgeting for. Then when you received your payday wages in cash you would divide the cash appropriately into the various envelopes. Each envelope contained the amount of money you could spend on that category of expenses in the coming month. If there was money left over from the month before, you had that much more to spend.

If you went to the "gasoline" envelope and there was no money, you didn't have any money to buy gas unless you "robbed" one of the other envelopes; say car repairs. If you robbed car repairs you wouldn't get into trouble, but you might not have enough money when the car needed new tires.

The "wallet" was a graphic way to keep you on your spending plan; keep you on budget.

Three Types of Budgets.

There are three ways people budget their money now: no budget, estimated budget, or exact budget.

Those who have **no budget** put their money in the bank and spend what they would like to spend, if it is available. They usually pay all their necessary bills at the beginning of the month and then just live off what is left until the next paycheck. They probably use the ATM card and check to see if they have money before they spend it. This method does work for some who choose to spend little or for those who have so much they can't spend it all. Those in the middle or those who run out of money at the end of each month would benefit from having a budget.

The **estimated budget** lays out the categories of spending and decides what you think you might allocate to various expenses. If you begin to spend more in one area than you estimated, you just spend more and take it from somewhere else, use a credit card, or take out a loan. This budget is just a guide for your spending, you do not have to follow it if you do not want to. This might be a good type of budget for a person starting to learn how a budget works but will not necessarily benefit you in the future when your income and expenses change.

Those who have an **exact budget** get to the end of their money in one category and do not spend more until they replenish the money at the next paycheck. Like the example of having the "wallet" with envelopes inside. They do not "rob Peter to pay Paul," as the saying goes. They learn to get by when they run out of money in one category and do not want to take money for the momentary event from something that should be saved for its proper use. An example: there is a concert you want to go to, but the tickets cost more than your entertainment budget can support at this time. So, you "borrow" from the food envelope, saying to yourself you will pay that back when you get your next paycheck and put less in the entertainment envelope for next month. But you often do not pay it back and the food budget suffers. Soon, you will only be able to afford Ramen.

A Budget with Explanations:

Category	**Things Included**
Income:	
Gross Wages:	Wages, Commissions, Pensions,
Other Inflow:	Interest, Dividends, Gifts, Alimony, Child Support, Rental Income, Welfare, Unemployment, Assets
Taxes:	Federal, State, Local, Social Security, Medicare
Contributions:	Religious Orgs, Non-profits, Helping Others
Net Income:	100% of the coins you put in your pocket.

Savings: The 1 coin	10% Set Aside for Reserve Account (3 months of expenditures), Investments, Retirement Accounts, Income Generation
Necessary Expenses	**Housing:** Mortgage/Rent, Insurance (Homeowners, Renters), Property Taxes, Repair and Maintenance, **Utilities;** Gas, Electricity, Water, Sewer, Garbage, Telephone, **Food:** for the house, meals out are Optional Expenses. **Clothing:** Dry Cleaning, **Transportation:** Bus tickets, Auto Payments, Auto Insurance, Gas and Oil, Repair, Car Replacement Savings **Medical Costs:** Health Insurance, Deductibles, Doctors, Dentists, Optometry, Counseling, Acupuncture, **Debt Management:** Credit Card payments, Revolving Charges, Loans, Notes
Optional Expenses:	**Insurance:** Life, Disability, Long Term Care, or Liability. **Savings**: for planned future purchases **Entertainment:** Eating out, Movies, Events, Recreation; Sports, Gym, Hobbies, Books, Magazines **Personal Care:** Hair, Nails, Allowances, Vacation, **Gifts:** Birthdays, Christmas, Hanukah, Weddings, **Other:** Cable Television, Cell Phones **Childcare/Education:** Babysitting, Day Care, Preschool, Private School,

	College, Tuition, Materials, Transportation

Another Method of Keeping Track

Just Write It Down.

Writing down what you spend is beneficial for several reasons. Take a piece of paper and write out your Necessary expenses; list the categories and how much you paid this month. Then draw a line to separate all the Optional expenses. As you spend optional money during the month add the name of the expense and the amount to the list. At the end of the month, look back over your spending.

Month:
Necessary: Rent Insurance Utilities Food Clothing Auto Medical Debt Management
Optional: Make a running list of things and amounts

When you look at the way you are spending your money you see where it goes, where you consistently over spend, where you can cut back on expenses, and you see things you might have to give up to have enough to spend on your Necessary Expenses next month.

Now you must ask yourself some hard questions for next month, especially if you did not have enough money to make it through to the end of the month. Am I spending my money the way I would truly like? Does my current plan help me achieve my long-term goals? What will happen if I have a major car repair? Will I have enough money set aside for the next health cost that might come my way?

Planning how you will spend your finances, saving for the future expenses that will come, and setting aside money to create Income Generators will help you reach your financial goals in life faster than the hit and miss tactics of those who approach finances without a budget.

Just a reminder. You will notice that Debt Management is a necessary expense because you have to pay the credit card bill or the loan you took out for the engagement ring. Once you buy something with a plan to pay for it later, the management of that debt becomes a Necessary Expense, you cannot avoid making the payment. It is an Obligation that reduces the amount of money you have in the future for Optional Spending.

An Alternative to a Budget.

Budgets are a lot of work. You spend a lot of time keeping records. Even if you do this using a computer program, and there are many programs available, it will take time to set them up and input the data. You will benefit from putting in the time. But it is time consuming.

The Alternative to the traditional budget is to develop a Focused Spending Plan; how you wish to spend your money. With this focused plan, you decide how much of your money you desire to spend on Necessary Expenses and how much on Optional Expenses. Then you spend accordingly.

You might choose to only spend 50% of your money, i.e. 4.5 coins, on you housing, food, clothing and transportation. That will free you up to have more Optional Spending. But it will also limit the number of places you can live, what you will wear, the food you buy, or how you will get to work.

A Budget is a Necessity

There is no right way to budget, but the people who have no budget or do not plan how to spend their money will waste it on things they do not need and end up not having what they would like to have.

If you work on your budget on a weekly or monthly basis, you will notice the out of control spending sooner rather than later. Just say you are spending too much on food. Maybe $50 a month. If you catch it in one money you just need to cut corners for the next two months to get back on budget. However, if you do not notice the overspending for 6 or 8 months, you are $300 or $400 over budget. You might not even notice this is happening until you must fix your car or pay your insurance bill and you do not have the money you need to cover the costs. It will take so much longer to get things right.

Some Thoughts about Cutting Expenses.

At some point, every person realizes they spend more money than they want to. They find out they are not making choices that will help them reach their goals. The first place to start getting things under control is with the expenses. Some people have the luxury of getting a second job or picking up more shifts at work, but you are exchanging your free time to cover expenses that you should have covered with the income you were making.

Finding ways to cut expenses takes a lot of creativity and discipline, but everyone can find ways to cut their expenses if they choose to.

A friend and his wife decided to never spend any money on Thursday. It didn't always work, but it helped them to curtail their overall expenses because they could not spend any money on Thursday.

Others take different approaches by not buying coffee at Starbucks but going to McDonalds instead.

You can buy the cheaper version of something, i.e. shop by price, but you should consider the length of time you will need the item, its value to you long term, and the quality you need so you do not have to buy it again.

Clothing might not need to last a long time because the styles do not last. Furniture might be fine now as used or thrift store, but at some point, in your life you might want something to last you a few years longer. Think about the cost of something and be willing to pay the right amount to get what you want for the time you will need the item.

You can spend less on car insurance if you raise the deductible or change the limits on the policy. Be careful you are not making unwise changes just to save money, but if your car is so old you do not need collision insurance, or you have enough savings to cover the higher deductible if you cause an accident, then by all means, spend the lower amount on the insurance.

There are so many ways to cut expenses in your budget. Most of them involve doing without. What are you willing to do without to reach your dream goals? Where are you willing to splurge to enjoy your present life? If you can keep those two ideas in balance, you will enjoy your life more, both now and later.

Credit Cards

Simply put, avoid Credit Cards. Some say you need a credit card to establish credit. To be successful in your finances, credit cards should only be used as a convenience and should be fully paid off with every bill. Otherwise you will begin to pay interest and then you might let the balance grow a little. Once the balance starts growing the interest mounts up and soon you have a large bill to pay off. That large bill becomes a Necessary Expense and eats into your monthly Optional Expenses.

This Page Intentionally Left Blank

Chapter Twelve;

Handling Debt

Top

The Profit & Loss Statement	The Balance Sheet
Active Income: Work Passive Income: Savings	Income Generators Savings/Investment Non-Income Generators
Necessary Expenses Taxes Charity Optional Expenses	Normal Liabilities Helpful Liabilities

When you owe someone money you become their debtor. They are your master, until the debt is paid. You have an obligation to satisfy the loan. Whether you are buying a car or a house and taking out a loan for the purchase, or you are borrowing from the bank with a credit card or personal loan, you are obligating some of your money, for a long time to come, to be used to pay back the loan. You are purchasing an Optional Expense by increasing your Necessary Expenses until the debt is paid off. You want to avoid that as much as possible.

Six Ways to Become Poor.

Since I am also a Presbyterian pastor, I get a lot of my ideas from the sage teachings of the Bible, from Solomon, Jesus, and Paul.

1. According to the Bible, **trusting money leads you to poverty.** How do you trust in money? It is quite simple, and it is more a mental thing than anything else. You believe that money will solve your problems, make you a better person, and bring you happiness. That is not true.
2. The second is like it. If you think **the solution to your problems is just having more money**, you will be wrong again. Another job, a higher paycheck, winning the lottery, betting on 14 at the crap tables, buying Crypto or betting on highly speculative stocks like GameStop. These desires for more money cause you to trust that your problems will be gone or minimized if you just have more money.
3. Being deceived by money is an easy thing. People become comfortable with their "nest egg." **"I have enough money and I will never have problems."** I remember so many people in 1999 who were thinking they could retire early and live the dream because the stock market was going up and up so fast. They were sure they had enough

to live on for the rest of their lives. Then the crash came in early 2000 and most stock accounts were cut in half or more. Then again in 2008 and 2022, stocks went lower. Every time, the markets have come back to the place they were before and went higher still. But, you never know how long your money will last.

4. **The buying power of money changes.** A certain amount of money will buy you a loaf of bread today and next week it might not. Look at the price of gas and how it fluctuates. You cannot plan out your costs for any length of time. It will frustrate you more than please you.
5. **Hoarding your money and trying to keep it to yourself will cause you to become poor.** Even though you think that building up your Income Generators will solve all your problems, if your life is not sufficiently balanced, you will end up poor; maybe not financially poor, but emotionally poor for sure. You need a balance of spending, giving away, and setting some aside for another day.
6. And as I talked about earlier in Chapter two, if you do not **learn to give to charity and generously share with others,** you will notice that the buying power of your wealth will dwindle away. If you honor God with your finances, learn to give it away to help others, you will avoid the poverty which you see in the lives of so many.

This Page Intentionally Left Blank

Chapter Thirteen:

Making Good Financial Decisions

Top

The Bible lays out 12 Principles of Financial Decision Making which wise people will benefit from;

1. **What I have on this earth is not really mine but is a gift from God.** Proverbs 3:4-6
2. **I need to humbly ask God and others for wisdom and help.** I Thessalonians 5:18
3. **I am better off if I generously share with others the resources I have been given.** Luke 6:38
4. **It is better to give than to receive.** The more I am willing to set aside my desires for the good of others the happier I will be. Luke 3:11
5. **Seeking to make a quick dollar will come back to bite me in the end.** Whether I am gambling on a win, or chasing a higher than possible rate of return, speculation will always be disappointing. Proverbs 28:22
6. **Pay people what you owe them.** Luke 14:28 - 30

7. **You are an example to others; they are always watching you.** Be honest and demonstrate integrity in all you do. I Corinthians 10:31
8. **Do not withhold what you have from the needy.** II Corinthians 9:13
9. **Never become obligated for another person's loan.** Never Co-Sign. Proverbs 6:1-3
10. **Live a modest, simple life.** Do not overindulge yourself in possessions and toys. I Timothy 6:8
11. **Learn to be content.** Whether you have a little or a lot, learn to be happy. There will come times of lack. Do not be surprised by them. Philippians 4:12-13
12. **Seek the peace of God, be settled in yourself.** Do not be anxious and troubled by this life. Proverbs 10:22

Chapter Fourteen:

Protecting Money

Top

Insurance and trusts can help you protect your money in a variety of ways. Insurance mitigates the risk and Trusts direct the transfer of money at the time of death.

Insurance companies were formed for two reasons; to make a profit and to share the risk of loss. Obviously, a company usually seeks to make a profit. Even non-profit companies need to make money from their work, they just can't spend the money to benefit the owners or officers of the company in the same way as a for-profit company can.

The risk the insurance company shares is this. They receive premiums from a large group of people and pay out money to members of the group if certain situations occur. If you are a member of the group and you pay in premiums, you are paying money in case you might have a need for it later; if you do not have the need you won't receive any payment back. If you are a member of the group and you have a need, you might receive from the company payments much larger than the amount of the premiums you have paid to the company. In this way, the insurance company is taking the risk for you. Your risk is limited to the amount of your premium, whereas the insurance company might have to pay for everyone. They calculate the potential risk and set the premium rate so that they can protect themselves, but they still have the risk that all members will have a claim at some point.

Some Different Types of Insurance.

Health Insurance covers some or all your health care expenses depending upon the conditions of the policy and what you are willing to pay for.

Life Insurance pays out an amount of money if you die while the policy is still in effect. It really should be called death insurance, but it would not sell very well. You can purchase life insurance for a shorter term to lower the cost or for a longer term up to your whole life. The longer the term of the policy the higher the cost because the insurance company has a greater chance of having to pay claims for you.

Liability insurance covers you when you do certain things wrong and the person harmed files a claim against you. This happens when you are in a car accident or someone falls on your property, etc.

Auto Insurance covers your car and the other car, your health and the other people's health, your

Liability and the other people's Liability depending upon who was in the accident and who was at fault.

Home-Owners Insurance covers the people who own the home when things go wrong, fires break out, or people get hurt on your property.

Renters Insurance just covers your possessions when you rent property from another person.

Funeral Pre-Planning Insurance pays for your burial costs when you die. Some people pay for this ahead of time so that the family does not have to be bothered with the cost of your burial when the time comes.

Two Trusts that Help with Protection.

Living Trusts and Wills, help you direct where your money will go after you die. With a living trust you name a trustee to take care of things after you die and this person oversees the disbursement of your estate according to your wishes set forth in the trust. Without a living trust your estate probably will end up in court and large legal fees might have to be paid before your heirs receive anything.

Living Will, which is sometimes called a **Healthcare Directive**, helps you predetermine how the doctors will handle your end of life health issues according to your desires even when you are not conscious enough to tell them. If you do not have the living will, the doctors are obligated to do and spend all that is necessary to keep you alive at all costs.

A person who is your trustee on the healthcare directive can also make decisions for you related to your burial plans. If you do not have a living will, the next of kin will handle all the burial plans.

Chapter Fifteen:

Having Money/ Retiring Well

Top

We cannot know that much about the future. We do not know what the tax rate will be when we want to retire. We have no way of knowing how much money we will want to spend in our last days. We do not know how long we will live or the condition of our health along the way. We could allow all this speculation to depress us or to motivate us.

We can, however, plan with all the tools at our disposal and create for ourselves certain Income Generators that will help us along the way.

How much do you need to set aside to generate income for you when you retire? Well, that depends on your dreams and wishes. Do you want to travel or play a lot of golf or ...?

A good rule of thumb says you need to have at least 75% of your current take home pay coming in when you retire. So, what are the sources of income you can expect in retirement?

Reduced expenses are a big help in retirement. One hope is your house will be paid for and you will not have the expense of rent or mortgage. You will not have to put money into your retirement account because you will be drawing from those accounts. Nor will you have to pay into the Social Security system now that you will be drawing from it, unless you continue to work.

Social Security is a major source of income in retirement if, as many people say, it is still around when you retire. Most people will receive around $2,000 per month. That is similar to having $600,000 in an investment account and taking a 4% draw every year.

Pension plans can be a source of income. Most companies are moving away from pension plans because of the management of these accounts becomes very expensive. If you have a pension plan from a past employer, you should have an income stream for life which may or may not increase in payout over time.

Retirement accounts are a good source of income in retirement. This is the reason you put the money into the accounts. You can draw from these accounts at about 4% per year. If your account is invested in stocks and bonds you should be able to take 4% per year for the rest of your life. As I mentioned earlier, 4% annual withdrawal from your retirement account will allow the account to last you 25 years, even if there is no interest being generated by the investments. Depending on the types of investments and the rate of return, your retirement account should still have money left in it when you pass away.

Time Horizon of Retirement Investments.

Many investment strategies suggest you should become more conservative in your investing as you get older. I disagree with this theory.

You want this retirement account to last as long as you do. If you are 65, retired, and beginning to draw or your retirement account, how long do you expect to live? The current life expectancy in the United States is in the mid-eighties. That means your time horizon is at least 20 years. If you desire to leave some of your money to your children, then your time horizon is more like 30 years.

You might reduce your stock portfolio and increase your fixed income but be careful not to be too drastic. If you used a 70/30 ratio for stocks to fixed income before you retired, you might go to 50/50 in retirement. Do not make the common mistake of reducing your stock investment to 0% because you want to “protect your money.” What you end up doing is reducing the return on your investments to below the rate of inflation; this reduces your buying power and makes your investment accounts unable to take you through to the end of your life.

This Page Intentionally Left Blank

Chapter Sixteen:

Starting a Business

Top

A lot of people think they can open a business by themselves and make enough money to live. However, 60% of all small businesses either lose money or break even. Let's talk about some ways to avoid being one of those statistics.

If you think you might like to own your own business someday, begin now to learn all you can about running a business. Think about some of the businesses you know that seem to be successful and go to work for them. A job at McDonalds or In & Out Burger might not seem glamorous, but they have a business system that you can learn a lot from. Go to work for them; start on the path to becoming a manager of a store and learn everything you can about running a business.

You might not desire to be in the fast food business your whole life. You are not choosing to be in the fast food business, you are taking a couple of years to learn everything you can about running a business well. How do you handle purchasing, advertising, sales, employees, company finances, and organization?

The Four Parts of Any Business.

To break down the structure of any business, small or large, you need four departments. In a small business the owner usually handles all four of these. In a larger business these become four divisions of the company. They are Production, Marketing, Finance, and Administration. Most people who choose to open a small business have an idea, and it might even be a "better" idea, but without all four of these parts of the business being focused on, the venture will likely fail. At the same time, most people entering business know one of these divisions well and maybe know a little about the other three. The time spent in a well-organized fast food company will give you a solid training in all four aspects of your future business.

Production,

The product of your business is what you have available to sell or offer to the public. It might be a gadget, a service, a food, or an item. Whatever you sell is your product and the part of the company that generates the product and makes it marketable is the Production Division. In the case of a convenience store type of business, you do not actually make the product but you do have to order it and stock it for sale. That is similar to production.

Most people who want to go into business have a "product" they believe will make them money. In most cases they are right. Their product might well be something others need, but without the other three parts to the business, the venture will struggle.

Marketing,

This part of the business is very crucial. This is where the product is taken to the market for sale. It involves packaging the product, advertising the availability, and in general, making the public aware that you have a product to sell or a service to offer.

Sometimes marketing is as simple as opening up a store front in a busy location and people will just come by to see what you have available. Most businesses today market on social media outlets and draw attention to their products. Other businesses use Radio and TV ads. Most service businesses grow based on "word of mouth" advertising. They just offer such a great service that their customers tell their friends about the service.

Whatever business you choose to open, you will not go far without some sort of marketing.

Finance,

Every business will deal with money in some form. The "product" needs to be purchased, the office supplies need to be bought, the office needs to be rented, and the workers need to be paid. Even if you are the person who offers the service and you work from home, you will have costs involved in doing the business. Then you will charge people for your work, your product, and the business will have income.

Part of the finance of a business is setting the price of the product so that it will not only pay for the cost of the production of the product but the other costs related to running a business as well as the profit needed for you to make a living.

Someone needs to keep track of the income and expenses so you can determine from month to month or year to year if you are making money or losing money. And you will need to report your income and expenses to the government in order to file your taxes. Someone needs to oversee the finances.

Administration,

The fourth part of business in overseeing the whole organization. When you are a small business and you are the only owner, you will stay awake at night planning your next steps. When the business grows larger and more profitable you might turn the administration over to someone else. But someone needs to take the lead in planning, organizing, and overseeing the work of the company. It is usually under the administration division that employees are hired, fired, and cared for. Once your business gets to the point that the owner is stretched too thin to make and sell the product, someone needs to take over the organization.

Types of Businesses.

There are five basic types of business organization and they will be briefly explained here. When you decide to start your own business, you should find someone to help you decide which of these business models you will use. They all have advantages and disadvantages which are best discussed on an individual basis.

Sole Proprietor,

This means you own the business and you will be the sole person running the business. You might have employees or independent contractors who help you, but it is your company. And the company probably does not generate enough sales to form a corporation, (200 to 300 thousand dollars a year).

Partnership,

This means two or more sole proprietors wish to work together at the same business. Maybe it is a service business that they all contribute to. Or it is a company that generates a product and each of you takes on a different role; product development, marketing, finance, administration.

S Corporation, S Corp,

This means a small business desires to incorporate to divert the Liability towards the corporation and away from the owner's personal Assets. An S Corp files its taxes and uses a special K-1 report to pass all its profits through to the owner(s) as income on their personal tax return.

C Corporation, C Corp,

This means a business that stands on its own. It pays its own taxes. All the expenses of the business are charged against the income of the business. The C Corp files its own tax return and the only thing the owner does is pay taxes on the wages they are paid as the owner. They might also receive dividends from the company and include those on their tax return.

Most Non-Profits are C Corps. The difference being the non-profit cannot in any way benefit the owners of the corporation other than paying them a salary for their services. All the profits of a non-profit must be used, kept within the organization, or passed on to another non-profit organization if your organization ceases to operate.

Limited Liability Corporation, LLC, or a

Limited Liability Partnership,

This means a business that is a hybrid between a corporation and a partnership/sole proprietor. The Liability of the owners is limited as with a corporation, but the LLC has the option of passing through profits and taxes to the individual owners. This entity can be flexible enough to offer better benefits to a single owner or small partnership than a corporation. See your state laws to help you decide if an LLC, LLP, or PLLC is right for your situation.

How to Have your Business Succeed.

Some form of **business plan** would be a good place to start. Your passion is not enough to make your business successful. As is stated in the book "Rich Dad, Poor Dad," anyone can make a better hamburger than McDonalds.

Having **enough money** is the next goal. If only 50% of small businesses make it after 4 years, then you should start with enough money to live on for four years. That way you can put all the profits of the business back into the company until you have a successful going concern.

Have the right **group of people around you** as you carry out your venture. They may not be working for you or with you, but have some advisors on your side. Listen to their ideas and let them listen as you struggle with new products or markets.

Are you aware of other people doing the work you are doing? **What is your competition?** And is your product priced competitively with the competition? You will need to find a balance between a price that will let you make a good profit and also let you sell your product competitively.

Have a **plan to market your product** to as many people as possible. Take a look at the percentages. If you have 100 friends, will you be able to market your product to all of them? What percentage of people will want to buy your product? What percentage will actually buy your product? Then determine how many items or hours of service you would have to sell to make a profit. That will tell you what the scope of your market needs to be. If one in 100 will buy the product and you need to sell 100 items a month to make a living, then you need to market to 10,000 people per month just to have a chance at making a profit. How often will people need to rebuy your product? Daily, Monthly, yearly, or is your product a one and done product? These types of questions need to be addressed as you enter into business. The Business Plan will help you with this.

Is the business dependent on the hours you put in? Are you offering a service that requires you to do all the work? Then you will need to make enough money per hour to pay all your costs and pay your wage as well. Are you selling a product that takes time to construct? Can others do that for you? Will you make enough money on each product sold to pay their wages as well as other costs of having a labor force?

Very seldom does a business succeed without spending time before you open the doors and continually as you run the business. It is not as easy as some believe to sell enough of your product to make a comfortable living. Most people who are successful in business have been in business before. This is not their first rodeo.

Conclusion:

These thoughts are just a few of the things I have learned along the way. Had I known these things before I was older, I might have made some better decisions in my life. My hope for all who read these pages is this:

That you would make better financial decisions and make them sooner because you know more about the basics of finances.

Blessings to you.

The Profit & Loss Statement	The Balance Sheet
Active Income: Work Passive Income: Savings	Income Generators Savings/Investment Non-Income Generators
Necessary Expenses Taxes Charity Optional Expenses	Normal Liabilities Helpful Liabilities

www.ingramcontent.com/pod-product-compliance
Lightning Source LLC
Chambersburg PA
CBHW050002230526
45465CB00003BB/1226

* 9 7 9 8 6 1 6 8 0 4 6 3 1 *